THE QUAKER ENTERPRISE

THE QUAKER ENTERPRISE

Friends in Business

David Burns Windsor

FREDERICK MULLER LIMITED
LONDON

First published in Great Britain in 1980 by
Frederick Muller Limited, London NW2 6LE

British Library Cataloguing in Publication Data

Windsor, David Burns
  The Quaker enterprise.
    1. Family corporations – Great Britain – History
    2. Friends in Great Britain
    I. Title
    338.7   HD2845

  ISBN 0-584-10257-7

Set in 10/12pt VIP Melior by
D. P. Media Limited, Hitchin, and
printed in Great Britain by
The Garden City Press Ltd.,
Letchworth, Hertfordshire

Contents

Illustrations

Introduction

The Quakers, members of the Society of Friends, have always been an intelligent and enquiring sect. Prevented in the past from entering the legal or academic professions, they sought other avenues of activity; instead of becoming pure scientists they became early technologists. Suffering persecution and constantly having their possessions taken from them, they went in for trade and manufacturing, where stocks could be replaced, and a business could be restarted overnight. They were a plain and sombre people whose preference for the garb of Puritan England led many to mistake them for Calvinists. They were very different from the rigid and inflexible members of that sect. Their love of their fellow-man, and their awareness of human weakness, led them to work for the betterment of society and the human condition. Swearing no oath, and signing no contracts, they insisted on plain dealing and their word was their bond.

The unpopularity of their opinions and the ostracism they suffered set them apart from society and this led to extensive intermarriage and large family networks, which were to have considerable influence in their chosen areas of activity in commerce and industry. The Quaker family enterprise was, indeed, to play a conspicuous role in the national economy of the Industrial Revolution and after. These enterprises were private, usually bearing the family name, wholly owned by members of the family, and usually entirely managed by them. The large Victorian family was capable of supplying a continuous flow of fresh blood to the 'firm' and with sons and daughters making judicious marriages, new partnerships could add fresh stimulus to the enterprise.

They flowered within two or three generations to become dominant influences in towns and cities across the country. Not all of them were

Quakers, but for those who were, there was the additional advantage of being part of a national network through which ideas, assistance, and business could flow. The scale of achievement of these Quaker enterprises is truly impressive and wholly disproportionate to their numbers.

Their interests lay, firstly, in raw materials – they effectively controlled the production and processing of iron, the basic requirement of the Industrial Revolution. Secondly, they had interests in manufacturing, controlling the manufacture of cocoa and chocolate products, and had substantial stakes in a number of others, including soap-making, pharmaceuticals, brewing, biscuit-making, china clay and shoemaking. They were also interested in communications and distribution, and were closely associated with the development of the canal and railway systems, and through them developed a whole system of commercial country banking that financed much of the local industrial development.

The result was to be a battery of household names, including Barclays and Lloyds Banks, Allen and Hanbury pharmaceuticals, Huntley and Palmers biscuits, Cadburys, Frys and Rowntrees chocolate, Bryant and May matches, Clark's shoes, Wedgwood china, Reckitt's 'Blue', Truman and Hambury's breweries. Eventually they became integral parts of Unilever, ICI, British Steel and British Rail.

It is hard to believe that these families did not hold industrial England in the palms of their hands, as the power they possessed would seem to have been a clear recipe for the operation of a conspiracy of influence. Yet the Society of Friends was a tiny sect whose numbers never amounted to more than one per cent of the population and who adhered to a strict code of principles. The conspiracy was one of friendship. The Quaker families never exploited their power.

The Victorian Quakers, as much as their modern counterparts, were great believers in the rights and dignity of the individual. They were aware of the extent to which they themselves had suffered from the self-righteousness of others. They detested exploitation and would have been appalled by modern corporate commerce with its low-risk, high-volume dull competitiveness. Their workers were generally better off than most, in both pay and conditions and, more important, were actively encouraged to take responsibility within the company for their own working lives.

The concept that allows each member the liberty of personal conscience is the essential ethic of the Society of Friends. It is voluntary – a commitment entered into gladly and freely. It is an association of friendly enterprises, never an organisation of ventures. There is no hierarchy, no 'Head Quaker', no layers of religious or secular chiefs – simply a loosely organised federation of autonomous meetings. There are regional monthly get-togethers, and even an annual meeting, but these have no powers to bind. As the Quakers never take votes, there is no possibility of committee rule, or the dictatorship of one.

Even their meeting-houses are secular rather than sacred. This has been the way for almost 300 years, demonstrating a remarkable strength for such a simple structure. This strength has been tested time and again by bigotry and misunderstanding.

The success of Quaker enterprise over two centuries is the more remarkable, given the assaults on the Friends during their early years of existence. The Friends were no small élite within the establishment of the country. Had they been members of the first families of the land, using resources of inherited wealth and influence, then their achievements would have been more comprehensible. Even at the height of their success they were not of the Establishment, but supporters of radical social policies and the Liberal Party.

The Quakers are not famous merely for their commercial enterprises, but also for their social welfare. Apart from the remarkable schemes at the workplaces operated by the Cadburys and the Rowntrees, they were associated with great advances in social welfare – penal reform, hospital care, educational development, housing schemes, the temperance movement and the abolition of slavery. As a Society they were prepared to court unpopularity to assault the evils of industrial England.

Finally, these men of commercial acumen and social conscience were also dedicated to their families. The love that breathes in letters from fathers to sons, daughters to mothers, is real.

We have taught ourselves to be cynical about our ancestors be they Georgian or Victorian. We regard both the eighteenth-century insistence on manners and style, and the heavy morality of the nineteenth, with equal distaste, seeing both as hypocritical.

The Quakers were of their time, their contribution governed by their particular understanding. The great Quaker entrepreneurs of last century were true Victorians. They stand out as members of the new, large, self-satisfied, self-righteous middle-class, who regarded themselves as the arbiters of a civilized society and administrators to a less educated world. They presented an austere and sober benevolence to the world. They were pillars of local society, comfortable in the knowledge of their own status. Benevolent they may have been, charitable and anxious to improve the lot of mankind, but it tended to be a fatherly benevolence predicated on a view that they knew what was right and good for people. Their image was inseparable from the ideal self-image of their time, they were people who conducted 'the practice of industry, frugality, temperance and honesty', and who were determined to be 'spiritual and solvent'.

CHAPTER 1

The Society of Friends

The Reformation of Henry VIII, for reasons which had as much to do with the needs of the English merchants as it had with his marital requirements, created the Protestant Church of England. Henry VIII had declared himself Head of the Church and as he was already Head of State the State and Church were as one.

Under his daughter Elizabeth I the concept evolved into a strict control over worship, a uniformity that continued unchecked into the Stuart period when the concept of the Divine Right of kings flowered into its truest expression. Whereas the Tudors were politically astute enough to operate this to their advantage, the Stuarts were not.

What had started out as a reaction to the excesses of the Catholic Church developed over time into something suspiciously resembling it – for 'Pope' read 'Monarch'. The dissolution of the monasteries and the appropriation of much of the wealth of the Church by lay landowners had deprived the Church of its capacity to provide its priests with adequate livings. This had created an undignified scramble for sinecures and benefices. The priest had to ingratiate himself with those who had the power to confer a benefice upon him and be ready to lie, forge, cringe and bribe. The growing excesses of the Church of England on the one hand coupled with its rigorous dictates on the other smacked altogether of the hated Roman Catholicism.

The Independents – many of whom were precisely the people who had gained from the original actions of Henry VIII – were established in the 1580s to demand greater freedom of thought and expression within a Protestant religious framework. They were not opposed to the monarchy, but the inseparability of the power and pomp of the Court from that of the Church made confrontation inevitable.

Only the monarch could grant religious freedoms, but the king had every reason to maintain the *status quo* – the one system that gave him effective control over his subjects. Only he could divest himself of the autocratic rights inherent in the concept of the Divine Right of kings. The Stuarts were firm believers in that right and had no inclination to alter it, James I making it abundantly clear that he opposed any reform of the Church. Opposition to the Church meant opposition to him and that was treason; opposition to him meant opposition to the Church which was not only treason but also blasphemy.

Independents represented the traditional puritan view that man was the author of his own destiny. They had power and wealth and had founded Sidney Sussex College in Cambridge, an expressly puritan foundation created on the site of an earlier monastery. The doctrinal influences of the College were radical: its students were expected to enter the Church and to abhor popery, all its manifestations and excesses. There were prohibited from having long or curled locks, great ruffs or velvet clothing; they were not allowed to frequent taverns, play dice or cards, bait bears or bulls or even play bowls.

The College was attended by the sons of the new class of landowners, traders, and craftsmen that the share-out of the dissolution had created. They, and the other Independents throughout the country, were resentful of the monarch and the Church. They demanded freedoms the king would not grant, abhorring the corruption and excess that he was responsible for sustaining. Among the graduates of Sidney Sussex, inheritors of the independent puritan tradition, was Oliver Cromwell, as significant a figure for the Quakers as he was for history. To the Independents operating within the Church were added Anabaptists from Holland who preached the right of individuals to worship in sects outside the Church of England.

The accession of Charles I brought a hardening of positions. Roman Catholicism under the Catholic Queen Henrietta Maria became fashionable again at Court and the trappings of Catholicism were added to the rituals of the English Church. Foreign policy under Charles continued to remain markedly pro-Catholic. This was anathema to the Protestants, being a threat both to their religious observances and to their freedoms as property owners and merchants.

At the same time the king needed money. The feudal system of financing the establishment and the ambitions of the monarch had long since ceased to function and the aristocratic landowners needed him as much as he needed them. Taxing the new money had proved to be the answer, but the price for this had been the establishment of a Parliament through which the levies could be raised. Parliament had to be recalled and the rising chorus of protest was presented with an opportunity to express itself directly to the king and his Court.

Cromwell was one of the representatives called to London, and as he and the others made their way to the capital, the air was charged with conflict. Resentment at the levy was high, the Dutch revolt against their Spanish overlords had fired popular imagination, and the fortunes of the Protestant League were followed with eager enthusiasm in England.

Into this ferment stepped Charles I preceded by an opening sermon by the Bishop of Bath to the newly assembled Parliamentarians, '. . . for though there be many pillars yet there is but one Unus Rex, one King, one great and centre pillar: and all the rest in the Kingdom do bear up under and about him.'

Charles I was not prepared to bargain for the money he needed: his position was not negotiable, and his rights were absolute. He needed money, and that was that. The Parliamentarians had other ideas and in response produced the 1628 Petition of Rights demanding the redress of such grievances as the arrest of subjects without trial and arbitrary taxation. Another response was the establishment of a House Committee on Religion. Though Parliament was subject directly to the control of the king, a Committee could elect its own chairman, sit as long as it liked, and speak as often as it wanted. The fact that the Committee was composed of the entire House was beside the point.

The Committee attacked 'creeping popery' in the Anglican Church. It was invited to adjourn, but instead it passed a resolution condemning popery and illegal subsidies. The king's appointed Speaker of the House was held down in his chair with the words: 'You shall sit till we please to rise.' The king dissolved Parliament and took upon himself the divine right to make laws and as a result Parliament was not to meet for eleven years. Those years saw the sowing and fermentation of revolutionary ideas of independent thought and action, of the democratic rights of man, of the laws of good and evil in society that were to shape the future evolution of society, and as a section of that nonconformist society the sect called Quakers.

Charles I and Archbishop Laud set themselves to crush the growing puritan element within the Church, and the nonconformist dissent that was developing outside of it. The infamous Star Chamber and the ecclesiastical Courts proceeded to repress all dissent. Academic freedoms were proscribed and the scope of texts on which sermons could be preached were drastically limited. Laws relating to censorship were arbitrarily applied, to extreme lengths.

Opinion was effectively controlled. No pulpit, lecture dais, debating chamber, or publication could be used as a vehicle to attack the monarchy. It was a bad time for England – one forgotten by those who point to the excesses of the Commonwealth. When in 1640 Charles was compelled to summon Parliament once more, the persecution of the Puritans, allied to hypocrisy and corruption, had tempered the resolve of a body of men to contain the power of the king as firmly as the king's resolve to sustain it.

These events led to the Civil War. The king was supported by the High Anglican Churchmen, the Roman Catholics and most of the English aristocracy. On the side of Parliament were both the puritan elements of the Church – the Presbyterians, the Independents, and also the Separatists, and the smaller landowners, merchants, freemen and burghers. The Catholic Irish were inclined to come in on the king's side, the Presbyterian Scots were prepared to assist Parliament, provided that Presbyterianism was established as the official form of Church government in England. This was accepted in the Solemn League and Covenant of 1643.

The New Model Army decided matters in the end. Whatever the political vested interests may have been, and whatever illusions of power existed, it was the army that became virtually the sole arbiter of events. Cromwell, whilst a Puritan, was determinedly non-Presbyterian to the extent that his army was deliberately officered by Independents, and in some cases, by Baptists.

This army defeated the Royalists army at Naseby – the critical victory of the Civil War. Later, when the Scots fell out with the Puritan Parliament, and allied themselves to the Stuart cause, it was again Cromwell's army who put the Scots to flight at Preston. Cromwell's insistence on freethinkers in his army was significant, not only for the future of Charles I, but for the establishment of nonconformism in England. Cromwell is presented by history as the ultimate puritan dictator, inflexible and lacking in humour. His New Model Army was the first organized power group of people who had neither wealth nor privilege. With the abolition of the monarchy, Church and State fell under the control of the army. It had never stood down between the wars, largely because of disputes over pay. The ranks were filled with freethinkers, malcontents, dissenters, religious mystics, political agitators and, above all, the Levellers.

The Levellers expounded a view representing an early socialism. Among their demands were universal male suffrage, the sharing of wealth and power, free education and public welfare. They attracted the disaffected elements, and a large portion of the army stood behind them.

When the army was finally invited into London to put down a riot it was further proof of where the ultimate power in the nation lay. It fired the desire of the Leveller element to control national events and the death of Charles Stuart and the establishment of the Commonwealth were the results.

These moves turned the New Model Army from one of right to one of might. As others before them had alienated their own supporters, so did the Army Council. Their attempts to impose justice and freedom made them tyrants, and in this way they alienated the independent-minded, provincial support which had created them.

So Cromwell became Lord Protector and England moved, as in so many revolutions, from Royal to Republican dictatorship, though every man in the nation had been shown a glimpse of freedom and there were plenty who were prepared to interpret freedom in their own way and to demand the right to do so. To the Levellers it meant the right to try to impose their interpretation of individual freedoms by force.

Everard and Winstanley took themselves to the common land of St George's Hill in Surrey and there, with a company of 'Diggers', established a commune whose philosophy struck deep at the heart of the prevailing concepts of property. Groups of individual 'seekers' after truth and light sprang up – Brownists, Baptists, dissenters and separatists, all preaching the principles of political, social and religious nonconformism. Into the midst of this plethora of ideas and actions came George Fox, a brilliant eccentric with much the same combination of passion and practicality as Cromwell himself.

George Fox was born in 1624, the year before Charles Stuart came to the throne. He embarked on his life's cause nineteen years later; his early life spanning precisely the period when the great events we have outlined took place. He came of good Protestant stock, his father being a weaver and churchwarden; his mother was also well educated and a devout Christian. Coming from Fenny Drayton in Leicestershire, they were precisely the sort of people whose interests the Independents represented. With all its other confusions the period was also one in which there was a migration from the land to the towns, brought about through agricultural depression. Fox was put as an apprentice to a man who was not only a shoemaker by craft, but also traded in sheep and wool and sold cattle. Through this Fox learnt an unusual combination of the needs and desires of smaller craftsmen as townsfolk, together with an instinct and love of natural freedom. By all accounts he proved skilful enough in trade.

Throughout this story of Quaker enterprise we are to see the common threads of technical skilfulness, practical business management, and yeoman instincts intertwined. These qualities were neatly combined in their founder, George Fox.

Fox was sixteen when Parliament was recalled and eighteen when the Civil War began. The king's standard was raised at Nottingham nearby. He was confused by the conflicting claims for religious and social morality, and sceptical of the Anglican Church. He set out a year later into a countryside already filled with every type and condition of itinerant – beggars, soldiers, refugees from one or other army, and preachers. His aim was to 'seek the truth' through the questioning of others and the inevitable contemplation of his own conscience.

It was three years later that he realized he had found the answer. He had achieved an understanding of truth founded on his own personal conviction rather than on outward received authority. To him that experience had the quality of a revelation. The light was within him: 'Mind that is pure in you to guide you to God.' He could divine the truth simply by addressing his own conscience. At the same time, through the realization of truth, came an awareness of evil in its many forms.

There is always a tendency to 'deify' spiritual innovators and much is made of this visionary period of Fox's revelations. It cannot be stressed enough that the social context of this period of his life must have had a critical influence. Thinking individuals, when faced with outward social disorder and contradiction, are inclined to fall back on individual solutions and this was by no means unique at that time. Fox himself saw this expressed as a universal tendency in the form of Jesus Christ.

In 1647, the year the army had marched into London and the great Leveller debates were held at Putney, Fox found himself in Nottingham. He was attracted to a company of Baptists and joined their number. Their outward practices, such as adult baptism, were matched by an inward principle that it was the right of any man to seek for himself God's truth in the scriptures. This right of individual judgement led logically to the belief that obedience to the State should not extend beyond conscience. The Baptists accepted that they should endure peacefully any punishments inflicted upon them as a result.

Placed in its social context, this set of ideas was understandable, and yet it is also understandable that such groups should provoke a powerful reaction. The concept of freedom from a national Church was totally alien to the seventeenth-century mind, and was seen as a revolutionary threat in precisely the way that socialism was seen in the early twentieth century.

The Anabaptists – a refinement of the Baptists – were the feared and despised bogeymen of their day. Anabaptism, based on the coincidence of the idea of individual religious liberty with the Calvinist view of a predestined elect, produced a 'holier-than-thou' concept that was seen as an intellectual perversion and self-indulgence. In particular the Presbyterians not only found Anabaptism heinous but also saw it as an inevitable abuse of the views of the Independents. Anabaptism had flowered in Holland as a result of the Dutch revolt, and thus had a further pernicious element to it.

The seventeenth century was a noisy and coarse time. Preachers, lecturers, and writers were not given to subtlety or cautious language. Throughout the first fifty years of the century the traditions of the sixteenth were maintained of using the most extravagant language to justify one's own cause and the most appalling vilifications to attack opponents. Fox was no exception. He believed in the power of direct action and his right to vilify evil. During his time at Nottingham he went to the justices at nearby Mansfield and called upon them to desist from oppressing servants' wages through the Courts. It is clear that Fox's message was by no means going to be restricted to purely spiritual considerations and that he sought a Kingdom of God on earth.

There were others with ideas of a kingdom on earth – in the form of the Commonwealth – and they were not prepared to allow alternative interpretations of the truth. As a result, in 1650, a year after he had left the Baptists to spread his message abroad, Fox was brought before Inquirers from the Army to whom he declared that he 'lived in the Virtue of that life and power that took away the occasion of all Wars'. He was taken away and imprisoned in Derby until the following year. Imprisonment for one's beliefs often acts as a confirming process, and so it was that George Fox on his release travelled throughout the North of England visiting and preaching to the many groups 'seeking after truth' in the relatively independent North West. He gathered to him a group of some sixty zealous believers who called themselves the 'First Publishers of Truth'.

George Fox was an imposing man, and it is impossible not to draw comparisons with the Lord Protector himself. He possessed the qualities of leadership, having a striking personality, a big frame, powerful voice and piercing eyes. He was abstemious and temperate. It was an age of the great preacher and man of action combined, both Cromwell and Fox possessing these qualities in abundance. Small wonder that Fox attracted a following and that he should earn the enmity of those he opposed. At Derby his action in calling upon Justice Bennett to 'tremble at the word of the Lord' was precisely the sort of behaviour that was to inspire his supporters to similar acts and infuriate others – particularly the Calvinists.

The period from the early 1650s to the late 1680s is characterized largely by the sufferings of the fast-growing sect that gathered around Fox. It is less easy than some Quaker historians suggest simply to ascribe these sufferings to their high moral principles in the face of a corrupt society. Certainly their beliefs brought them into direct confrontation with the authorities, but we have to recognize also the effect of both the behaviour and the popularity of the Friends on attitudes towards them.

There is little doubt that the zealous followers of truth – these

'Children of the Light' — were also a confounded nuisance and as a source of civil disturbance they took over where the Fifth Monarchy men had left off. There was a strong hysterical element in the early manifestations of their beliefs and enthusiasms that was feared by magistrates and justices.

The pacifism and quietism associated with the Quakers belong to a later period in their history. The early Quakers deliberately caused disturbances once they had been 'moved' by the Lord to interrupt a church service or preacher. To stand up and accuse priests of being lackeys and hirelings, to call them corrupt and deceivers were not acts calculated to provoke a moderate response in the puritan age. Stories abounded of the Quakers trembling and howling, trance-like in their revelations, evangelical in their passion to share their experiences. Today similar young enthusiasts for religion who behave in much the same way in America are known as 'Jesus Freaks' and this aspect of early Quakerism cannot be ignored. The repressive responses of an authoritarian society are understandable. The Quakers were described publicly as people deprived of all modesty, morality and civility 'running from Assembly to Assembly troubling the Ministers'.

Even Cromwell was to be treated to exasperating displays of Quaker philosophy. Fox was brought before him in 1654, having been arrested yet again. The great man was impressed by Fox and his views, for the meeting ended on a cordial note. Fox was then invited to eat in the Protector's Hall which he promptly refused. Other Quakers were to come uninvited to Whitehall to convert or merely to berate Cromwell. It says much of the Protector's tolerance that he was prepared to stand and listen to such attacks on himself.

It was not only their civil disobedience, carried out in twos and threes, and often carefully prepared, that provoked the authorities and often other Christians. There were a number of other manifestations of their deeply held beliefs that were to be received with hostility. Terms such as 'your honour' and 'your worship' were to be reserved for God alone, so they addressed magistrates or churchmen simply as 'Sir'. They refused to take their hats off to authority (in common with other Leveller groups) and above all refused to take oaths.

All Christians, they argued, are specifically directed by Jesus to 'swear not at all' but, secondly, to swear to tell the truth implied that one was not bound to do so. This double standard was unacceptable to them and they regarded their word as their bond. This led them into difficulties when required to take the oath of allegiance to the State, or later to the Crown. It also gave the authorities a classic device for bringing them to book.

A further source of trouble for the Quakers was their refusal to pay tithes and much had been made of the Friends' persecution on this account. The whole issue of tithes strikes at the heart of seventeenth-century society, for it marks the sticking point in the revolutionary programme of the Commonwealth. The Quakers were not the only group opposed to tithes – the entire Leveller philosophy in the army was based on their abolition. But to the authorities, the abolition of rents such as tithes was the first step towards the abolition of property itself. The Puritans may have been concerned to see that the management of the country was placed in the hands of the godly – once having given property to the elect they were certainly not going to see it handed over piecemeal to anyone else. It is impossible to underestimate how deeply this question of tithes went to the heart of men's convictions at this time and how passionately views were held on both sides. Even today the question of property rights, when they conflict with human rights, still produces heated emotions. For the early Quakers to demand the right to dissent not only from the established Church, but from an essential element in the property system was inviting trouble indeed.

Trouble they got, and in refusing to pay tithes they laid themselves open to the very people they had provoked and outraged – the clergy of the Church of England. Their stand on this issue gave persecuting vicars and rectors, afraid of the freethinking independent Quakers who refused their ministry and attacked them as lackeys and hirelings, an opportunity to have them fined and imprisoned.

The fines were invariably exacted in the form of a restraint on Quakers' goods and property. This was an open invitation to legitimized thievery and goods valued at ten or twenty pounds would be seized for a tithe of only a few shillings. It is a matter of history that when minority groups are persecuted public consciousness is at best neutral or indifferent. The Quakers by their public provocations were not initially very popular, inviting scorn and the resentment of those less able to stand up and demand freedom and liberty.

Since 1650 Fox had started the great tradition of Quaker itinerant preachers. As the small groups of Friends established themselves often in adversity in towns throughout the kingdom, the need for communication was acute. Preachers like Fox would bring comfort and spiritual regeneration to Friends who would often have lost everything. They brought news of the sufferings of others and, more important, news of their success in overcoming their persecutions. They were the creators of new groups of Friends through the power of their oratory and the instinctive appeal of their message.

In 1651 Fox had travelled on foot some 750 miles through the North of England and gathered together an initial group of some sixty zealots who called themselves the Friends of Truth. These 'disciples' travelled the length and breadth of the country and in four years created over seventy-six settled meetings in the North and fourteen in the Midlands.

Their habit of travelling made them visitors to towns, and therefore more vulnerable to persecution, especially when their anti-social antics invited trouble. A charge frequently used against them was made under an Elizabethan Act 'for punishment of rogues, vagabonds and sturdy beggars'. The travelling preachers were easy prey for a magistrate seeking to give an object lesson to local townsfolk. The zealots were whipped, put in stocks and imprisoned.

In 1655 Cromwell was forced to allow the passage of an Ordinance that prohibited the disturbance of ministers and other Christians in their assemblies and meetings. It was to give even greater power to those who sought, or were sometimes forced, to punish the Quakers, and their sufferings grew.

Under Cromwell some 3,170 persons were imprisoned, whipped, put in stocks, or otherwise abused for being Quakers. Thirty-two had died. Under the restored monarchy the situation worsened for the Quakers and in 1661 a detailed tract was drawn up showing that more than 5,000 people had been similarly punished under the king, of whom twenty-two had died in prison. 'Figures quoted by the Quakers, who were careful only to recount provable cases, tend to be conservative. It is likely that anything up to twenty thousand people suffered persecution during the time of the Restoration and at least 450 died as a result.

Refusal to swear oaths, to give honour to the Establishment, or to pay tithes, meant blasphemy, treason and sacrilege to a seventeenth-century world that was all too well aware of such possibilities – revolts in Holland and the English Civil War gave every excuse, and even justification, to fall on small groups of Independents who obstinately and publicly opposed the Church and the State. The persecution of these groups led to a moderating of their wilder, informal, zeal and a more careful consideration of the question of organization and modes of conduct.

Out of the fiery upheavals of revolutionary mid-seventeenth century England grew the more recognizable body of men and women in their plain clothes with their rigorous personal honesty, and quietist and pacifistic attitudes who were to create the great Quaker enterprises of the next two centuries.

The tradition of keeping careful records was born during the period of suffering. There can have been few more devastating documents presented to king and Parliament than those which carefully listed specific cases of unfair distraint of goods, or unjust imprisonment, for example:

> Cumberland. Anno 1662. In this year Adam Robinson, William Bond, John Richardson, suffered about seven months imprisonment having been arrested for Tithes at the suit of Francis Howard of Corby . . . who afterwards at the Assizes obtained judgement against them for treble damages upon which were taken from
>
> Adam Robinson for a demand of £1. 5. 0, four beasts worth £28. 0. 0.
>
> William Bond for a demand of 7s. 0d. a mare and a steer worth £3. 15. 0.
>
> John Richardson for a demand worth £1. 12. 0, cattle worth £7. 10. 0.
>
> A total of £39. 5. 0. for demands of £3. 4. 0.

Joseph Besse's 'A Collection of the Sufferings of the People called Quakers for the Testimony of a Good Conscience' for the period from 1650 until the Act of Toleration of 1689, stands as one of the most extraordinary documents detailing individual events in history that can ever have been compiled.

Through Margaret Fell, a Cumberland sympathizer, another aspect of the Friends developed: the holding of business meetings. The Friends had held religious meetings on Sundays as an inevitable consequence of their beliefs, and, in order to keep together, they had tended to meet once during the week as well. Other meetings were organized for Elders to discuss the business of the Society, and these were held monthly. Larger meetings were held more occasionally on a regional basis. Through these Margaret Fell collected and distributed monies to pay fines, care for and maintain the families of Friends in prison, and pay the travelling speakers. The regional meetings, held quarterly, quickly became a regular feature of the Society's activities, and in 1660 the first annual meeting (to consider the sufferings of Friends) was held at Skipton in Yorkshire. This structure of Sunday religious meetings, and monthly, quarterly and annual meetings has survived over 300 years. More important than illustrating the durability of the simple structure of the Society of Friends, is the fact that out of these meetings came the features readily recognizable in the conduct of Friends in business.

The Quaker practice of holding the greater part of their meetings in silence came as much from civil disobedience as it did from members quietly seeking inner light. The words of members as they 'trembled and called upon the Lord' could clearly be taken and used against them. The practice of assembling and enduring verbal and often physical assaults in silence was not only dignified, but an effective way of avoiding further trouble. The words and deeds of man are always open to external control, the thoughts of man are not, and the silent dignity that developed during the period of their persecution probably ensured the Quakers' survival.

The lack of priests and dogma and the practice of contemplation forced the Friends to a degree of self-awareness and discipline that is essential in the entrepreneur. The tradition of inner strength to cope with both the assaults and temptations of their external world certainly was partly responsible for creating the great Quaker entrepreneurs.

The practice of meeting at local and regional levels, and travelling in the ministry – a notable characteristic of the Friends – produced a close-knit group of genuine friends with strong personal ties. The inevitable discussion and mutual assistance was to become one of the great strengths of the trade groups that developed in the various industries in which Quakers were involved, leading to the creation of partnerships in industry and considerable intermarriage at a time when families tended to be large.

The Quakers, therefore, were born and grew in adversity which was partly of their own creation but ultimately because of the circumstances of their times. The Quaker Act, the Conventicle Acts, the Corporation Act and the Test Act not only caused persecution and suffering for the Friends; it also excluded them from the universities and from the professions.

The Corporation Act, which was to remain on the statute books for over two hundred years, meant it was impossible for Quakers to enter the traditional trades and crafts of the older corporate towns. Even in the non-corporate towns they had enormous problems. By refusing to take oaths they effectively precluded themselves from the judicial system. They were unable to sue for their debts, defend themselves or give evidence. Nor were they able to prove wills or be admitted to copyholds. Finally, their own scruples kept them from entering into trades concerned, for instance, with fashion, such as tailoring, or lace-making. They would have nothing to do with arms manufacture, nor would they accept goods from ships protected by arms or dealing in slavery.

It seems inconceivable that members of a sect so persecuted and labouring under such difficulties could even contemplate going into business as traders and manufacturers; yet they did and from the start they had certain advantages. George Fox and his earlier colleagues represented a careful, thinking and often intellectual element in the nonconformist Protestant movement. Education, the law, politics, the military and the trade guilds being denied them, their intellectual experimentation and observation was channelled into business, producing a high calibre of trader and manufacturer with a predilection for technical development and the application of scientific principles to the production of commodities.

The Quakers, religiously and socially, had chosen to reject corrupt worldly distractions and to live simply, frugally and honestly. Every waking moment was to be seriously occupied in activities that were 'a service to truth, honesty and mankind'. They adopted the typical Protestant ethic: wealth for its own sake was a sin, work for its own sake was a virtue. Simplicity and economy were to become their trade mark.

Anxious to demonstrate the validity of their faith by integrity and trust, the Quakers became famous for providing goods of quality at a fair price, inventing and producing better and more useful articles, keeping to their word over delivery dates. They began fixing their prices long before it became customary and ultimately these derided people with their despised religion took their place as trusted and valued members of the local community. The consistency of Quaker success in business throughout the country led in the eighteenth and nineteenth centuries to the evolution of a network of Quaker interests which, in terms of both its complexity and depth, had enormous potential power.

CHAPTER 2

The Quaker Connection

The Quaker enterprise found its seed bed in the Industrial Revolution – more important Quakers were responsible for many of the crucial events, one of the most important being the development of a new method of producing iron. This technique removed dependence on wood in favour of the more abundant coal, and through the application of a recycling process of water, using steam pipes, turned the mills into full-time producers of iron.

As a result iron flowed to build the steam engines, produce the manufacturing machines, lay the rail tracks, construct the bridges and build the ships that stimulated Britain's development as the world's first industrial economy.

At the centre of this advance were the Quakers and they came to dominate the iron industry. The key family was the Darbys of Coalbrookdale who developed the use of coke and applied steam pumps to recycle water. Three generations of this family were to transform the Shropshire countryside with their foundries, tracks, and canals, turning Coalbrookdale into a Mecca for Europe's applied scientists and engineers, and leaving behind them a monument to the craft – the Iron Bridge.

Another Quaker family was to dominate the smelting, processing, distribution and sale of iron goods in the area around Birmingham, a town which was itself to become a symbol of both the Industrial Revolution and the new independent, nonconformist provincial Britain. Their name was Lloyd. Starting in the seventeenth century with a small forge, they became so comprehensive in their role as ironmasters that they found it advantageous – as well as profitable – to establish a bank to provide short-term credit to their many customers. That bank was to develop into a whole new banking system, making use of local traders' money rather than that of the investors of the City of London.

The Quakers found metal-working of all kinds congenial to their scientific and inventive abilities. Apart from becoming goldsmiths and silversmiths, they were prominent in the lead industry, forming the London (Quaker) Lead Company, and, even before the Darbys came to dominate the iron industry, playing an all-powerful role in the brass industry, centred principally around Bristol. Such was their monopoly in this field that Parliament was petitioned in 1771 with the complaint that all the wholesalers in Britain 'could only buy kettles in Bristol at whatever price they care to charge'.

Quakers were also responsible for the world's first railway. In 1814 George Stephenson visited Edward Pease in Darlington, a Quaker stronghold. The Peases, who were Friends, had been most successful combers, weavers, and wool-buyers, and their success had led them into collieries and banking. Edward Pease was faced with the problem of transporting coal from his mines at Auckland to Stockton and Darlington. Should the shipment be by canal or in trucks hauled along an iron railroad? Stephenson proposed that Pease should use the latter, and told him that he himself had developed a locomotive worth fifty horses. 'This is my Blücher', he said, comparing his iron horse to a famous racehorse of the time.

Pease was convinced, and this innovation was to lead to the world's first passenger train, which travelled on what was called 'The Quaker Line'. Consisting of six waggons loaded with coal and one coach with directors and friends, the train did the twelve-mile journey to Stockton on 27 September 1825 in just over three hours. The time taken included a number of stoppages, no doubt for celebration. When Pease died there were 7,000 miles of railway in Britain.

Quakers were also responsible for the method of financing the railway. Pease, in association with two other Quaker bankers, Jonathan Backhouse and Thomas Richardson, raised the money by issuing a prospectus to the public, and this became the standard way of financing new railways, as it was of the canal system. In virtually every such speculation – and the word should be understood in its nineteenth-century context – Quakers were to be found among the promoters, often acting as bankers or treasurers. It may seem surprising to find sober, austere and pious men 'speculating' in this way, but it will be seen that the risks were minimal when it is realized that the railways invariably ran close to, if not through, Quaker enterprises. The Lloyds even had a canal diverted from its projected course for this reason, and men like Joseph Crosfield sat on the board of railway companies whose lines ran across land sold to them by Quakers.

Enlightened self-interest was as much a hallmark of Quaker speculation as it was of Quaker enterprise.

Joseph Rowntree was a director of the Midlands and York Railway Company, Joseph Crosfield of the Great North Western. The Lloyds were involved with the construction of the lines that took the first trains from London to Birmingham and Liverpool. Francis Fry, a member of another famous Quaker family, was a director of the Bristol and Gloucester and the Devon and Cornwall Railways. James Ellis, the Quaker MP for Leicester, was chairman of the Midlands Railway Company. James Cropper was an active promoter of the Liverpool and Manchester Railway. These and other Quakers were involved with other railways – the Liverpool and Manchester, the Birmingham and Derby Junction, the Midland Counties and the North Midland, the G.W.R., the L.&N.W.R., the L.N.E.R., and the Midland Railway Company.

The railways also needed experts to run them. One of the mechanical geniuses of the early railways was Charles May, a Quaker who had worked in the engineering section of Ransome and Rapiers, the great East Anglian agricultural combine – another Friends' enterprise. He and Ransome patented an essential device for fastening rails to sleepers. It was also a Quaker, Thomas Edmonson, who devised the railway ticket and its associated stamping machine.

Then, of course, there was that bible of railway timetables – Bradshaw's Railway Guide. George Bradshaw was probably the best-known and most popular of the Friends who were associated with the early development of the railways. He first produced his Railway Guide in 1839 and until 1939 his world-famous book *Bradshaw's Railway Times* was distinguished by its use of the Quaker habit of calling the months by numbers, January being known in the guide as 'the first month'.

Famous Quaker names stand out when we turn to the porcelain and English china-clay industries. Three such names remain with us – those of Cookeworthy, Champion and Wedgwood.

William Cookeworthy, the greatest of these, died the poorest. He was an innovator, and an inventive genius, who never ceased his studies, largely unaided by the experience of others. He began life as a chemist and in common with many another Quaker he turned to the practical ways of applying his scientific knowledge. He settled in the West Country and began explorations to find the kind of clay which could be used to manufacture genuine porcelain. He discovered kaolin – the 'china' clay – in three different places near, St Austell and entered the market with porcelain made in England of entirely native material.

He did not at this stage make a great deal of money, perhaps because he lacked the customary Quaker flair for organizing markets or because the 'market' still needed educating to the idea of purchasing china. Eventually he sold his interests to Richard Champion, whose family had connections with the Bristol brass industry and the Midland and South Wales iron industries. Champion began to produce china of artistic style and quality, and it began to sell. The industry was secretly extended when a Shropshire syndicate purchased licences under the guidance of the man who was to become the most famous of English potters, the Quaker Josiah Wedgwood.

A great deal of Quaker enterprise went on in the provinces and Quaker families were centred on, and came to be associated with, particular towns or counties, sometimes representing them in Parliament. As we have seen, the Darbys were based on Shropshire, the Champions on Bristol, the Peases on Darlington. The Lloyd family were connected with Birmingham (as were the Cadburys), the Crosfields with Warrington, the Rowntrees with York, and the Palmers with Reading. John Bright, the radical Quaker orator, not only represented Rochdale, where he developed the family enterprise of cotton manufacturing with his brothers, Jacob and Grattan, but he was the first Quaker to become a minister of the Crown. The Brights' business extended to spinning, weaving, bleaching and dyeing and to the manufacture of carpets, and by 1847 the firm employed over one thousand workers.

It was not only the Quaker ironmasters who encouraged marriage within the Society. Members of the Bright family married into the Clarks – a large West Country Quaker family who were to leave Street in Somerset and become famous as shoe manufacturers in Northampton. Another marriage brought together the Brights and the Barclays, a Quaker family of Essex and Scotland.

The name of Barclay stands with that of the Lloyds as one of the pillars of the modern commercial banking system. Their banks came into being originally not as funnels for investing capital, but to service the growing demands of provincial trade. The Lloyd family were doing business with so many traders in the iron business that they set up a bank to provide short-term credit for their customers. The concept of providing such credit to trade is as old as moneylending and many banks owe their early origins to the lending of 'seed money' to farmers. It was the Industrial Revolution that stimulated demand for credit, and Quakers all over the country were there to provide it.

There were a number of reasons for this. First, many Quakers had become goldsmiths, and as such were natural people to leave money with, as their premises were secure and their security obvious. Secondly, the Quakers had an impeccable reputation for integrity, plain dealing, and honesty that was unique in the eighteenth century.

Lastly, they were also obsessive book-keepers – indeed, recorders of everything that ever happened to them.

The Records of the Society of Friends are as complete an account of the affairs of a single group of people as it is possible to find. They are comprehensive memoirs of the life and times of several generations. Originally, they were started in order to record the sufferings of the early Quakers, the fines and sequestrations of Quaker property, and to arm their fight for justice. The practice reveals a fundamental instinct of the Friends. They are practical people whose beliefs are locked into the real, day-to-day world as much as the world hereafter. They are committed to keeping their affairs in order; indeed local meetings would often inspect the records of Friends in financial trouble in order to advise or help them, and they were happy to serve others in administrative and financial capacities.

The country banks became as important a feature in sustaining the Industrial Revolution as the developments in iron were in creating it. Had it been left to the London financial houses tied to the practice of an earlier age, it is doubtful if the necessary speculation would ever have taken place.

The history of one of the most successful of the families of country bankers serves to illustrate the way of the Quakers in finance. The Gurneys were an old family who had come over originally with William the Conqueror. They settled as landowners in Norfolk, where they grew to have considerable influence. They made good use of the land, and apart from rearing sheep they became wool staplers and substantial spinners of worsted yarn.

They went into financing around 1650 and no doubt were concerned in the provision of loans to buy seed, lease land, and purchase implements, reaping their returns when the harvest came in. Over the next hundred years their financing interests outstripped their other activities, and in 1775 John and Henry Gurney formally established the Norwich Bank. Their sons and grandsons carried on the business, one of them usefully marrying into the Barclays.

Bankers providing local credit in exchange for notes and bills of exchange ended up with a pile of paper and no money. Thus they would have to wait until the bills matured before they could lend money again. Consequently, the banker would himself sell the bills to someone else for a discount. He could realize a quicker, if somewhat smaller, profit on his loan and have his money back to lend to someone else. Country bankers had a particular need to turn their money over quickly and were forced to go to the City of London to discount their bills with brokers. The Gurneys were no different, but they went one stage further, establishing their own bill-broking business, which was to become the greatest credit insititution in the financial centre of the world.

The new firm dealt in commercial paper in the widest sense of the term. They were innovators, introducing a system of charging a commission of one-quarter of one per cent to the borrower instead of the lender. This became a standard practice in financing and it still obtains to this day.

The Gurneys associated with two other Quakers, Overend and Richardson. The latter was a cousin of the Peases, and had started work as a messenger boy in another Quaker bank, Smith, Rice and Co. He was to become the manager of Smith, Rice and then went into business on his own account. Forty years later he had done so well that he was one of the bankers of the Darlington Railway venture.

Railways made his fortune – lines like the Stockton-Darlington Strip, engine works in Newcastle, companies like the Great Northern Railway. He was known, in fact, as 'Friend Rothschild', his outward austerity concealing his substantial wealth.

He then went into partnership with John Overend, another Yorkshireman, who had started his working life working for another Quaker concern that had progressed from wool to finance, the firm of Smith and Holt.

The bill-broking business was a marriage of Norfolk and Yorkshire interests, encompassing the traditional trading of wool and the progressive development of the railways. The operation of Messrs. Overend and Richardson, involving young Samuel Gurney, was established in 1797. Gurney was no novice at the profitable discounting of bills as the Norwich Bank had been conducting such business through another London associate for some time.

Gurney brought other factors to the enterprise – connections that would be the envy of the City. He was related to the Barclays, to the Buxtons – a family of influence in East Anglia to this day – and to the Backhouses, another Quaker banking family. He himself married Elizabeth Shepherd, who possessed a vast fortune of her own and he was brother-in-law to the Fry family, known for banking as well as chocolate manufacture. His status is underlined by the fact that he was a co-founder of the British and Foreign Fire and Life Assurance Company. His partners were Nathan Rothschild, Sir Alexander Baring (Lord Ashburton) and Sir Moses Montefiore.

This demonstrates not only the obvious power of individual Friends but the way in which their interests overlapped, the role of intermarriage in promoting alliances, and their obvious willingness to enter into partnerships with other members of the Society.

The new enterprise was very much a 'banker's bank'. It also created within the City an independent unit offering an alternative to that bastion of the financial establishment, the Bank of England. Bankers could deposit their surplus funds with the Quakers instead of going into government stocks.

Overends were, indeed, to become the most important establishment in the greatest financial centre of the world – the ultimate answer to those who question the individual power achieved by the Friends. Not only had Overends succeeded in the provinces in raw materials, manufacturing and financial services, but also at the centre of the establishment. By 1856 the Overends held eight million pounds on deposit, while Alexanders, another Quaker company, held four million. By the end of the decade Overends were making half a million pounds profit a year.

Their enterprise was, however, too large and too concentrated. The heirs to the early Quaker caution and practical business sense were less responsible than their forebears and the whole lot came crashing down seven years later in one of the great financial catastrophes of the century.

The Quakers reached their zenith in the 1860s. The Friendly enterprises had stamped their mark on the economic life of the nation, but were all, inevitably, to hit the same reef; as private ventures they were too big for one family to maintain personal liability. The Joint Stock Acts were just around the corner and the day of the disinterested external shareholder was about to dawn. Even before these Acts the Quaker companies were appointing managers and directors from outside 'the family'. The third and fourth generations of Quaker entrepreneurial families simply could not deal successfully with the complex structures their fathers and and grandfathers had developed.

In many cases the grandsons and great-grandsons were less than interested in fighting the good fight. They inherited success and received the best education – the education of young gentlemen – and they chose a way of life very different from that of the early Friends; many indeed left the Society for the Church of England and the Conservative Party.

The family enterprise, however, did not disappear or change overnight. Many, like the Cadburys, retained an essentially Quaker image well into this century and, indeed, many great Quaker 'names' are still with us today. Despite the end of the Overend, Richardson and Gurney bill-broking business, Alexanders continued and are still, along with the United and the National Discount Houses, a major concern in financing.

The real monuments to the Quakers in finance are, however, the commercial banks, Lloyds and Barclays. David Barclay stands with George Fox and William Penn as one of the great founders of the Quaker approach, though Barclays Bank, unlike Lloyds, has not evolved as a single linear unit.

So far our somewhat random roundup of Quaker wealth and influence has demonstrated that any litany of ironworking, railways and country banking will be largely composed of Quakers. If that were not enough, the Quakers were doing as well in a host of other activities and in one case ensuring as comprehensive a presence as in any of the above.

Georgian and Victorian England has been castigated for its gin-soaked urban classes but it is probable that the gin was scarcely more lethal than the water. Throughout history ale had also been a more lively form of refreshment, and brewing was regarded as an activity worthy of pursuit by any man of God. Cromwell's own family included brewers.

What was good enough for Cromwell was acceptable to the Quakers and in spite of the fact that they became prime movers in the temperance movement, they saw nothing contradictory in brewing ale. John Perkins of Southwark, for instance, worked for Mrs Thrale in a brewery on the site of Shakespeare's Globe Theatre. Mrs Thrale was advised by Dr Johnson to sell to a consortium consisting of Robert and David Barclay, John Perkins and Sylvanus Bevan who was the first chairman of the newly formed Barclays Bank. To this day Barclay Perkins and Co. has retained a Barclay, a Perkins and a Bevan on the board and appropriately the symbol of the brewery has remained a bust of Dr Johnson.

Just as well known is Truman, Hanbury and Buxton's brewery linking banking and pharmaceutical interests. There have been many other Quaker breweries – the Lucases of Hitchin, the Rickmans of Lewes. If the connection between banking and brewing appears unusual, the Quakers were not unique. A recent chairman of the Bank of England, Lord Cobbold, similarly came from an Ipswich brewing family.

The other major area of Quaker influence was in foods and confectionery. The Quaker names in this field are famous because they have become brand names. Three of the family enterprises that achieved international fame were those of the Rowntrees, Cadburys, and Huntley and Palmers. They had much in common, apart from being Quakers. They dominated the towns in which they operated, but their activities stand as text-book business ventures and yet, almost more important, as models of industrial relations and human management. These names are probably the most often-quoted examples of Quaker enterprise and the fact that they exist today – as enlarged, public conglomerates, with a host of household brand names – is a justification of their methods. The dominance of Cadburys and Rowntrees in cocoa and chocolate manufacture is awe-inspiring.

Nor were they the only Quaker manufacturers to create household brand names. The company of W. H. and J. F. Horniman was founded in Newport, although in 1852 it moved to London. John Horniman himself became a great philanthropist, particularly in the field of international peace and arbitration. Although J. Lyons and Co. were to take the company over in 1918, Horniman's Tea has retained its distinctive brand name and style.

The story of the young Joseph Crosfield – son of a grocer – and his creation of what evolved into a soap and chemical giant, bringing names like 'Old Brown Windsor' soap and 'Persil' to the British housewife, also contains all the elements that run throughout the Friendly enterprise of the eighteenth and nineteenth centuries.

Isaac Reckitt acquired a recipe for making starch in payment for a bad debt. It was unusual, because it used sago and not potatoes – very significant at the time of the Irish potato famine. He took out a patent and his son James took over its wholesale manufacture in 1856. The Company became a tremendous success and, within twenty years, £500 worth of founders' shares were returning £4,000 a year. Reckitts have grown into a major conglomerate, and their enterprise over the last half of the nineteenth century is another model of industrial relations.

James Reckitt desired, like Joseph Rowntree and George Cadbury, that working conditions should be as pleasant as possible. He determined that his workpeople should be secure in their employment, protected against illness and accident, receive pensions in their old age and share in the profits made by the company. All of these, except perhaps the last mentioned, are accepted today as fundamental rights of workers – not so in Victorian England. Reckitts 'Blue' became a household essential, and as closely identified with starch as 'Swan Vestas' had become with matches. In fact, Bryant and May, another Quaker family business, became part of the British Match Corporation, but not before they had amassed a capital of two million pounds. Today, Bryant and May are still traded as a distinct venture.

The extensive Quaker family of the Clarks hailed from Street, in Somerset. Marrying into other Quaker families and inventing a machine for turning out hexameter verse which scanned, they went into business. The Clark name figures in partnerships around the country but it is their enterprise in shoes, slippers and galoshes for which they are best known. To this day Clarks shoes are a byword for reliability and quality in Britain's High Streets.

Other enterprises with which the Quakers were associated include: Price Waterhouse & Co., the eminent company of auditors, who were originally Quakers, and J. Walter Thompson, the world's greatest advertising agency, while Joseph Lister, the great surgeon, was born and educated a Quaker and represents a stream of great Quaker doctors and surgeons.

The world famous pharmaceutical enterprise of Allen & Hanburys began with the Bevans, an old Welsh family that can be traced back to William the Conqueror. Sylvanus Bevan left his home in Glamorgan in 1714 to seek his fortune in London. He was far beyond the average apothecary of his day in learning, and the business he opened in Lombard Street was unique: he stocked only drugs of the best quality, selling them at a fair price at a time when there was much abuse in the dispensing of drugs.

Sylvanus believed in jumping in at the deep end. In the year that he completed his apprenticeship and started the pharmacy he also married Elizabeth, daughter of London's famous clockmaker, Daniel Quare. In 1731 he was joined by his brother Timothy who began developing the interests of the company overseas.

The Bevans intermarried, like good Quakers, particularly with the Barclays and the Gurneys, neither of whom could have done the business any harm. Brother Timothy's son, Joseph Gurney Bevan, paved the way for the enormous growth of the company in later years, and invited William Allen, a chemist, to join it. Allen's interests extended to languages and physics, and the result was that the pharmacy became a centre of scientific research as well as a business.

The happy combination of rigorous business principles with progressive concepts of applied science underlay many of the ventures of the Quakers. Their lively minds could not ignore the theoretical basis of their activities, and they applied scientific principles to the development of their processes. Their insistence on proper apprenticeships produced men who were sufficiently well versed in first principles to allow for successful experiment and innovation, and their strict business practices, prompted by a determined Protestant morality, ensured that their developing products were efficiently marketed.

Thus it was that the Friendly enterprise, that confederation of Quaker family partnerships, spread across the face of Victorian commercial England. They attained enormous power as individuals but chose to use that power for the benefit of their employees, their local community, or their industry. Never did it occur to the Quakers as a body to use their undoubted power to advance their own interests. The proof of this lies in the achievements of Quakers in activities where the only motive could have been the common good.

The stories of the individual Enterprises which follow illustrate in particular settings many of the general qualities so described.

CHAPTER 3

The Lloyds of Birmingham

Dolobran lies a few miles north of Welshpool. It is a house and estate, built in the fourteenth century by Celynin ap Rhiryd, lying in the valley of the River Vruwy which runs into the Severn. The first person to take the name Lloyd, which means grey-haired, was his great-great-grandson.

Two generations later, the first Lord Powys, a Royalist, lost the manor, having backed the wrong side in the Civil War. The manor house was occupied by a Commonwealth commissioner and the Lloyd family were moved into a smaller house on the estate. Lord Powys's son, Charles Lloyd, re-acquired the house in 1651; however, his enjoyment of the restored fortunes of the Lloyds was sort-lived, as he died six years later. It was left to his son, Charles Lloyd II to administer the estate 'left to his own disposal'. He was, in fact, forced to leave Oxford without a degree in order to do so.

Although the Lloyds were not wealthy, they were gentry, and Charles Lloyd II was an attractive prospect now that he had taken his father's place. He was invited 'to court several persons of noted families', but he went further afield and married Elizabeth Lort, the daughter of a wealthy Pembrokeshire family.

Charles and his wife settled into the routine demanded of local nobility. Charles became a Justice of the Peace, and was offered the post of High Sheriff of the County. He was probably unable and certainly unwillingly to take up such a role and the responsibilities involved, and chose instead to concentrate on the estate. Charles set about making his estate pay by felling and selling substantial quantities of timber and by constructing an iron forge. Iron forges were being built all over the country as a result of the decline of the iron industry in the Sussex weald. Traditionally iron had been smelted in the great oak forests of the South-East, using a charcoal-based process. This use of forest wood clashed with the demand for mature oak for ship-building. Many of the iron forges had been destroyed by the Royalists during the Civil War, and the area had declined as a centre for iron making. Consequently, small local forges (such as that at Dolobran) were springing up wherever there was a conjunction of ironstone and afforestation. From that small forge grew a mighty dynasty in iron and ultimately a second dynasty in commercial banking.

No story of the Quakers is as simple as that, for Charles Lloyd himself was to undergo suffering and privation and his sons were to inherit little but their father's honesty and determination to stand by principles.

In 1662, they had become acquainted with a group of the then despised Quakers and had attended a meeting conducted by an itinerant Friend. Worse still, they invited everyone present to their home.

Such an action must have caused something of a sensation in the locality. The aftermath of the Civil War was not a time to be associated with the freethinking, anti-Establishment, rebellious Quakers. For someone appointed to uphold the law to consort with such people was doubly treasonous.

News of the meeting travelled fast and Charles Lloyd was summoned with those others present before Edward, Lord Herbert, Baron of Cherbury. They were asked to take the Oath of Allegiance and Supremacy. The Quakers refused such requests on the grounds that to do so implied a double standard of morality. To the socially nervous Establishment, such refusals were an affront, and when Charles Lloyd joined his friends in refusing to swear, he was committed to prison with them. Elizabeth chose to join him in prison where they suffered badly. Thomas, a brother studying law at Oxford, petitioned the justices, claiming that Charles had not been tried and eventually he was removed to confinement in an empty house.

They were to be confined in that house for ten long years, sustained by the goodwill of friends. Their own goods were under distraint; much had been forfeited and sold; their home was neglected. The promising world of the young Lloyds was in ruins but their commitment to the new faith was deepened by their imprisonment.

The Declaration of Indulgence of 1672 brought their release from confinement, but Charles was to suffer fines and distraint for another thirteen years. He travelled widely in the ministry before settling in Birmingham, a town much favoured by Quakers on account of its non-corporate status which did not require a tradesman to be a freeman. Charles died in 1698, his family committed to the Society of Friends. His brother Thomas Lloyd had also suffered fines and imprisonment before joining William Penn in America and becoming

President of the Council and Deputy Governor of the state of Pennsylvania.

The children of Charles Lloyd needed no reminding of their parents' suffering, for they were born and spent their early years in the house where their parents were imprisoned. The two boys, Charles and Sampson, were to marry before their father died to daughters of the same man, Ambrose Crowley. He was an active Quaker, who had started in business as a blacksmith and nailer and had built up an extensive business dealing in iron and ironmongery in London and the Midlands.

It is an interesting sidelight on the speed of growth in Quaker family business that Ambrose Crowley's son was knighted for his enterprise in establishing an international iron business linking Sunderland and Newcastle with Sweden and Danzig. It is also clear that the Lloyd boys had married into a substantial business connection.

If that were not enough, Elizabeth Lloyd, the daughter, also married well, into the Pemberton family, whose interests were in iron and goldsmithing. The Pembertons were intermarried with no less than three other iron-making interests.

By the time the Lloyds celebrated their fiftieth anniversary in the iron business, they controlled extensive interests in the production and distribution of iron and ironware in the Birmingham area. They did so through a large family and numerous intermarriages.

It was the family of Sampson Lloyd, Charles's younger son, who took the first steps towards the creation of the bank that is a household name today. Sampson's son and two grandsons decided that they would enter into a partnership with a relative, John Taylor, who was a button manufacturer, and with their cousin, John Pemberton. They chose to go into banking, and to fully understand that decision we must be aware of two or three related factors. First, the Lloyd interests, together with those of their related partners, constituted a considerable network, and internal financing was becoming a necessity. The Quakers, historically, had little faith in 'outsiders' and were unlikely to want to put their finances in other hands. Indeed, there was such a tradition amongst the Friends carefully to record all their business transactions that they were natural husbanders of anyone's money.

In the seventeenth century, the function of bankers was restricted largely to the provision of personal loans and accepting the custody of personal valuables for safekeeping. Quaker goldsmiths had a natural advantage in their transition to bankers. The mere fact that they worked in gold meant that they could underwrite any notes they issued to merchants for goods they held on their behalf. Merchants would then use these notes to obtain short-term credits.

The Lloyds' cousin Pemberton came from a family of Quaker goldsmiths and John Taylor's family had been silver workers. To add to this, there was a small army of local manufacturers and traders who did business with the Lloyds and who needed short-term credits to stimulate their businesses.

The Seven Years' War was over and a spirit of expansion and improvement was abroad; it was a good time to go into banking. Birmingham, nonconformist and freethinking, was a pivot in this expansion. Free of the social constraints that operated in London, this provincial centre was a natural magnet to the self-making entre-preneurial families exploiting the opportunities provided during the Industrial Revolution. A new collective consciousness was develop-ing among the second and third generations of these entrepreneurial families. New projects abounded and subscriptions were being raised for every kind of major scheme.

Taylor and Lloyds Bank was opened in Birmingham on 3 June 1765 with a capital of £6,000 held in four equal shares. They accepted deposits from individuals in five-guinea and one-pound denomina-tions. Later, to counter the shortage of small change, they issued seven-shilling notes (which were, of course, one-third of a guinea).

They also operated local credit through a device known as the inland bill of exchange. This was a forerunner of the cheque and comprised both an undertaking to pay a given sum of money and directions for how it was to be paid. This bill, containing the names of both payer and payee, could be made payable 'on sight' or at a later date, say, thirty or sixty days later. In the intervening period, the bill could be employed as a source of value, form of saving, or payment to a third party, or for raising cash through discounting the bill – selling it for slightly less than its face value to someone who would cash it in later.

The venture, opening in Dale End, which was at the end of Birmingham's short High Street, had working arrangements through Sampson Lloyd with credit centres in London and could thus discount bills on a substantial scale. Taylor, too, had many connections in London. In fact, both Sampson Lloyd and John Taylor were really too busy to attend to the day-to-day running of the bank and so this was left ot the junior partners, Sampson Lloyd III and John Taylor III. The older men lent their reputations and their experience, supplying many contacts and maintaining connections in London.

Their contact and agent for bill discounting in London was John Pocock, a factor in Queenhithe, and dealer in corn and iron. He was to assist Taylor and Lloyd to complete a remarkable coup just five years after the establishment of the bank in Birmingham. Taylor and Lloyds, the country bankers from the Midlands, established a branch in London, a reversal of the normal process. The success of their operations in Birmingham had given them a power base from which they could compete with the Establishment in London.

The move was exceptional. There were barely a dozen banks in the whole of England outside London, and in every case they were correspondents of factors like Pocock. This was not enough for the Lloyds; they wanted a bank in London, and with the help of two new partners they went ahead. The manager of the new venture was William Bowman, the other new partner was Osgood Hanbury, who had married Sampson Lloyd's sister, Mary. He was a successful tobacco broker from Essex and had connections with South Wales iron interests through relations in the Crowley family. The Hanburys were also to be involved in the establishment of Truman and Hanbury's brewery and their further connections with the Barclays gave Osgood first-class contacts in the London financial brokerage.

The Lloyds' iron interests underwrote this venture and the flow of cash created at Dale End gave further security. Neither of these required a London extension and it must be asked why these provincial non-conformists desired to compete in the Establishment's own power centre. The answer lies in a clearer understanding of the social and economic context in which the Lloyds were operating. Across the country, the Quakers and others had established major primary industries in coal, iron and steel, cotton and wool, chemicals and foods. These industries spawned secondary ventures into manufacturing for the growing consumer markets that the employment of labourers, clerks, and managers was creating. The success of the primary and secondary phases of the Industrial Revolution depended upon something further – the efficient movement of goods and people at every stage of the process of production and distribution. The development of a transport system was not only essential, but also an extremely attractive proposition to investors. The Quaker entrepreneurs who had established the industries that had created this demand were also fully aware of these new possibilities.

The canal that had carried the Duke of Bridgewater's coal across to Manchester was short and simple but it fired the public imagination. It was cheap, creating higher profits, and it was efficient; in short, an entrepreneur's dream. It certainly caught the Lloyds' imagination for, as one Lloyd put it, with enthusiasm: 'Let town be joined to town – markets to their supplies. Let sea be joined to sea linking the leading ports of London, Bristol, Liverpool, and Hull. Let the Thames and Severn, Mersey and Trent all be joined by water.'

The Lloyds of Birmingham were determined to be in the forefront of the development of canals. They had a network of iron foundries, smelting mills and blast furnaces. If they were linked by water, their connections with both customers and suppliers would be streamlined, meaning a cheaper and more efficient service.

In 1771, a year after the establishment of their London bank, we find the name Lloyd appearing on the management committee of the new Birmingham canal. The canal led directly to their country iron-works at Powick and Burton. The canal formed part of a three-way link with the Severn and the Trent, and would soon be linked with London and Liverpool. Taylor and Lloyds were the bankers to the canal company and a Lloyd was the treasurer.

No doubt, as Quakers, they achieved such things as a result of their outstanding honesty, but such achievements were also clearly to their advantage. The existence of a London bank gave them even greater opportunities in the raising of investment finance and the discounting of major bills due to these speculations.

The key figure in these developments was the younger Sampson Lloyd. He was entering the busiest period of his life. He had succeeded in establishing two successful banking ventures, which were central to the general development of the Lloyd interests. Enjoying considerable civic status, he was required to act as one of Birmingham's street commissioners who were established by Act of Parliament in 1769 as the town's principal regulating authority. Sampson also underwrote the debts of the new hospital in Birmingham.

If the demands of town and business were not enough, Sampson had family duties to perform. He looked after his uncle Pemberton's property at Wednesbury, he managed the estate of his cousins, the Sandrettes, at Bristol, and he also assisted his relations, the Wilkinsons, who were elderly and childless. In the year that the new bank opened in London, Sampson had to spend an inordinate amount of time rescuing his cousin Pemberton from a mountain of debts.

By the mid-1770s Sampson Lloyd was entertaining no less a personage than the great Dr Johnson, accompanied by Boswell. Johnson had connections with Quakers in London through his interest in a brewery that had been purchased by Osgood Hanbury. No doubt he had been commended to visit Sampson Lloyd, or as Johnson puts it: 'We next called upon Mr Lloyd, one of the people called Quakers. He was not at home but his wife was and received us courteously and asked us to dinner.'

Johnson enjoyed the intellectual company of Quakers but had little time for them as a sect. This was to lead to a ferocious argument with Sampson over the question of infant baptism. They agreed to differ, with Johnson claiming 'I am the best theologian but you are the best Christian'.

Sampson headed a growing family dynasty. His seven children had all married other Quakers and he was to have forty-four grandchildren, who in turn, produced no less than 120 offspring.

Sampson Lloyd and his partner, John Taylor, had achieved business and social respectibility on a scale undreamed of by their grandfathers. Only ten years after opening the bank in Birmingham, both this and the London bank were doing exceptionally well. They were however coming to the end of their lives. John Taylor died in 1775, a loss keenly felt by Sampson, who continued to watch over the success of their business until his death in 1779. His obituary described him as 'a gentleman of the strictest probity and unsullied character'.

The company had to be divided equally between the Lloyd and Taylor families. The eldest sons, also named Sampson and John, were already members, owning a quarter of the shares each. The death of Sampson meant the inheritance by his grandsons, Charles and Nehemiah, of his quarter of the shares and they joined their father to make up the Lloyd half. John Taylor's shares went to his son who already held his own quarter. Taylor was, therefore, now a man of substantial means.

Charles and Nehemiah were very different characters. Charles, a man possessing the Quaker virtues of accuracy, honesty and precision, had been trained in the bank at Cheapside and was to take over the private ledger of the company for no less than the next fifty years. Of Nehemiah there is less to be said. He was not a banker, nor inclined to be one. Personally, he was irresolute, lacking in drive or initiative. After several unhappy years he was politely returned to the Lloyds' iron interests where he could be more easily absorbed.

Nehemiah, in a sense, was a catalyst in the resolution of a growing conflict between the Lloyds' iron and banking interests. The money business was burgeoning but the great days of the iron business were passing. Nehemiah was to die at the turn of the nineteenth century, some twenty-five years after the death of his father. That last quarter of the eighteenth century saw the peak and initial decline of the Lloyd interests in iron and his death precipitated much discussion about the final winding-up of these interests. The Lloyds were anxious to make their way into the nineteenth century free to concentrate on their banking business. To wind up their iron interests was no easy matter. Over the previous quarter of a century these interests had become complicated. They had developed a substantial complex at Powick. Side by side stood a rolling mill and a slitting mill. These were flanked by a coal yard and wharf to which the pig iron was delivered for processing. In addition, there was a barn, a carpenter's workshop, a blacksmith's and stables. There was a house with a garden for the manager, and a row of cottages for employees.

Over at Digbeth their slitting mill was producing 1,200 tons of rod for nails and they held a significant holding in the shape of a forge at Burton and its associate mills. The Lloyds were part of a consortium which owned transport and water rights on the River Trent at Burton. This gave an edge to their trading power, as they had immediate access to cheap transport and through a link-up just below Burton to a major canal system. During the 1780s steam power had been added to the processes at Burton. Newcomen's 'fire' engines had been refined sufficiently for use in iron works. The new versions were called 'common engines' and were fired by coke which made them cheaper, cleaner, and more efficient. It was typical of the Lloyds, as Friends, to opt for practicality whilst at the same time absorbing themselves in the complexities of the new technologies.

It should not be forgotten that the Lloyds would have had the advantage of being part of the tremendous interchange of ideas that was taking place in the Society of Friends and, being free of the political and structural constraints operating elsewhere, they were able to liberate new scientific and technical ideas in the form of innovation in their iron businesses. Yet always there was practicality, and in letters written by Charles Lloyd, manager of the plant at Burton, there is an anxious attention to the performance of individual cylinders and worry if a flywheel would be too heavy for its supports.

Despite technical progress the business was, however, becoming uncompetitive. Whilst certain plants like the one at Burton were amenable to technical improvement, others were not as they were becoming worked out and inefficient. The rapid expansion of plant at Burton, Digby and Powick had involved considerable credit at the bank. By the end of the century the iron interests were causing the Lloyds some embarrassment. The Society, which took an interest in the business affairs of members, frowned upon anything that looked like irregularity or misdealing, and it was clear that the problem of overfunding the iron businesses could not be resolved.

From the start of the nineteenth century they began systematically and in a businesslike manner to divest themselves of their un-profitable iron interests. Nehemiah's death in 1801 was followed by the disposal of Powick to Thomas Elwell, a Birmingham iron master. The stock of the iron merchants' business they held in Edgbaston Street was sold to their competitors, Gibson and Co., in Birmingham, and the slitting mill Digbeth went to a man called Tomlinson. The sites surrounding these premises were sublet to tenants. Burton was disposed of in 1812. They obtained the consent of Lord Uxbridge, upon payment of £800, to remove their equipment and to convert the premises to cornmilling which was then sublet to other interests. The forge was also sublet. With typical practicality, the business was dismantled in a way that was to reduce the indebtedness of the company to modest levels. The firm's account was finally closed in 1815, and it brought to an end that great first chapter of the two-part

Lloyd story, leaving their interests solely in the bank in the nineteenth century.

The ending of the Lloyd interests in iron working was also the begining of a period that saw the lessening of Quaker unity in the families' interests from a time when everyone was a Quaker to one in which some were not, and in which the family developed associations with notable figures of the age who were not themselves Quakers. It could be argued that this represented a coming of age for the Friends, since they no longer had to depend upon each other. Moreover, with the Lloyd family multiplying by 300 per cent per generation, religious and family unity was becoming progressively harder to maintain and liaisons outside the Society were inevitable. In the nineteenth century there were great areas of activity – a flint mill in Leicestershire, coal and other Black Country developments, and family interests in literature and science – but the Lloyds are best known for their bank.   The Industrial Revolution was in full spate, with enormous growth of towns such as Birmingham. The city had doubled in size during the previous forty years, now housing some 70,000 people. Country banking was prospering; in some ways they were better placed than the London houses. Their underpinning was local trade and commerce, with a burgeoning new consumer market in the same workforce which was creating the wealth. They were less inclined to be nervously affected by international events. The onset of the war against France had caused several London banks to crash and in 1776 the threat of invasion had caused another run, resulting in the refusal by the Bank of England to give gold in exchange for their own notes.

The Birmingham banks survived this. The Quakers' refusal to invest money in war, as well as their continued practice of honouring their notes on demand in the domestic market in which they primarily traded, no doubt actually strengthened their position. We know that the original partnerships of two Sampson Lloyds and two John Taylors had been altered by the deaths of the older Sampson and Charles. These had been replaced by Nehemiah and Charles Taylor on the one side and by no one on the other. Yet another Sampson (with his brother, Samuel) was brought in in the 1790s to assist his father (the younger Sampson, who was now over seventy) at the Birmingham end of the business – he would be Sampson Lloyd IV. In the winter of 1800 both this new Sampson and the errant Nehemiah died. So, in 1802, Charles's son, James, was introduced and in 1805 the single Taylor was supplemented by his son James Taylor, aged only twenty-two. The greater burden was falling on the Lloyds and, although Taylor held half the equity, at this time he took only forty per cent of the profits.

There were distinct branches of the Lloyd family in Birmingham at this stage. There were eleven brothers and sisters, including Sampson IV and Samuel, in the Sampson Lloyd family at Bingley. The Charles Lloyds had seventeen children, including James, and lived at Farm. Two of these on the male side, Sampson and Samuel, went into the bank in Birmingham. Another went into the bank in London, two others into other banks held through the Barclay connection. It would take a book, or perhaps a television series, to chronicle the story of these two families. Much endeavour was made by both families to maintain Quakerly traditions and to keep errant sons and daughters in the fold.

They were largely successful in as much as many members of the family had reputations as honest, plain-dealing contributors to society as family men and businessmen. Both families carried on the Quaker tradition of intermarriage, often marrying into families which their antecedents had already joined in matrimony. It must have been a nightmare to those many chroniclers of the history of Friends when trying to construct family trees. The Sampsons married into the Braithwaites of Kendal and the Harmons of London. The Charles Lloyds married into the Fosters of Bromley (shortly to feature in the bank). James, who joined the bank, was temporarily engaged to Elizabeth Gurney, later to become Elizabeth Fry, but James eventually married into the Harts, a Nottingham family of bankers. Charles Lloyd's eldest son (not destined to become a banker) married into the Pembertons who had figured in the early Lloyd marriages. It was Charles (of a somewhat romantic disposition) who became acquainted with Lamb, Southey, and Coleridge and was much affected by the Romantic philosophies of the day. Although Friends may see Charles as turning away from the Quaker tradition, there is much in the almost pagan Romantic literature that is in essence not dissimilar to the Quaker view of inner light. Indeed, Charles's eldest daughter, Priscilla, married William Wordsworth's brother, Christopher, who (horror of horrors to her father) was a clergyman in the Church of England. Robert, the other brother to be influenced by the Romantic poets, eventually compromised and became a bookseller and also married a Hart from Nottingham. Finally, other members of the family married into the Whiteheads (another Quaker banking family) and into the Bettensons, not Quakers, but of substantial position in Ipswich. Not only did this gregarious family establish literary relationships with Lamb, Southey, Coleridge and the like, they apparently also established a relationship with the painter Constable, since no less than six of their sons and daughters, with their spouses and children, were painted by him. That fact is interesting in itself since two generations earlier the Quaker's plain dealing would permit few pictures, if any, to adorn their homes. Charles Lloyd, the sire of all these offspring, was plainly embarrassed by this affectation and would not be painted himself.

The economic unease of the late eighteenth century continued into the nineteenth century. Many country banks were opening and, although the early establishments were now well founded, many of the newer ventures failed. There was more than a smell of control in the air and the Lloyds at Birmingham often found themselves involved in deputations and meetings to protect the interests of the country banks. Prominent were James Lloyd and his new brother-in-law, Paul Moon James, a personable young Quaker banker in Birmingham and part of that family of Galton and James who had purchased the iron business in Edgbaston Street. James and Paul, in their letters to the now elderly father, Charles Lloyd, reflect the extent to which they were in touch with the lively local interests and politics of the day in Birmingham and the political developments in London that were affecting their interests. The restlessness of the common people in towns and the scent of reform were abroad when P. M. James acted as chairman of the town's principal public committees. He was a member of the lobby that spoke in London to the Prime Minister, Lord Liverpool, when, in 1818, the country banks were threatened with a restriction on their rights to issue notes.

In 1814 John Taylor had died and had been replaced by his second son, William. George Lloyd (from Farm) had also been added to the list of partners, now numbering six, in 1821. In 1825 the great financial crisis broke, causing enormous runs in the branches of the country bankers. Resourceful as ever, the Lloyds (Samuel, in particular) had foreseen the emergency and overnight shipped substantial sums of money up to Birmingham by post chaise. They withstood the run whilst some sixty banks went under elsewhere.

Charles Lloyd, careful keeper of ledgers for over fifty years, died in 1828. Having painstakingly steered the Lloyd enterprise in the stormy first quarter of the nineteenth century, like Sampson Lloyd before him and the original Charles Lloyd, he had displayed precisely those qualities required by the family interests at the right time. He had consolidated the family fortune through the pruning of uncompetitive ventures and the establishment of new partnerships and financial interests. He had taken the bank up to a new form of organization, joint-stock banking, and the creation of the modern Lloyds Bank. This came at a time when the problems of containing the bank under the six partners proscribed by law might well have threatened its future.

Charles Lloyd, the devoted businessman and family man, was just as involved in local society and philanthropy as Sampson had been. In his will he left legacies to the Birmingham General Hospital and the

British and Foreign Bible Society, formed in Birmingham and supported by many Friends. His funeral was a public occasion; the
meeting-house was too small and the assemblage stood quiet in the
street. An eye-witness counted twenty-eight carriages.

The Lloyd family like to refer to the events of 1856 as 'the Great
Change' but there were forty years between Charles Lloyd's death and
this date. Those forty years were characterized by enormous tensions
and changes in the Lloyd family, and not a few in the bank itself.
There were two important alterations to affect the bank at this time; the
right of country banks to have more than six partners, provided they
were more than sixty-five miles from London, and the Bank of England. This had come about because of the failure of so many banks and
the lack of sufficient partners to bear these losses. It was also required
that such a bank should be organized as a joint-stock enterprise, thus
holding all stockholders liable. Limited liability was still to come and
joint-stock banking meant the loss of the personal touch characterized
by a partnership.

Since such service and the status of the partners were such a
cornerstone of the Lloyd enterprise, they decided to continue with the
six partners and risks they understood. In so doing, they also avoided
the problem of differential status of the Birmingham bank and its
London bank which as a merchant bank really depended on the status
of its partners. The arrangement that the Lloyds and the Taylors
should hold half the shares each remained and in 1830, the partnership consisted of James and William Taylor (the sons of John the
Younger) on one side and Samuel (son of Sampson) with his offspring, George, and James (son of Charles) with his offspring, Francis,
on the other. Francis had been admitted on the death of his grandfather, Charles, with impeccable Quaker references. He went on
shortly to become High Bailiff whence, no doubt, his public status
inspired a wicked summons by an eccentric for malpractice in the
bank. Through carelessness by his own lawyer, he was found guilty,
but later reprieved when perjury was proved. By this time he had
resigned from the bank.

George Lloyd, the other youngster from the Sampson Lloyd herit-
age, was another to spend half a century in the bank. A partner for over
thirty years, he was not the 'front man' that Sampson and Charles
had been, or Francis would have been. He was a banker pure and
simple who understood money and how it moved. He was a source of
great security to the bank's customers, providing the all-important
continuity at a time when great changes in the town of Birmingham
were taking place.

The town was given borough status. It now had over a quarter of a
million people, a new town hall, and a market hall. The new railways

coming from London and Liverpool were linked to Birmingham in 1837 by the opening of a railway station at Curzon Street to the east of the town. In five years, the second station at New Street was opened and within another five that at Snow Hill, causing the removal of the Quaker burial plot containing all the Lloyds to a new site in Bull Street. In 1840, William Taylor died at roughly the same time that Francis Lloyd resigned. There were no more Taylors, so James was left with half the holdings of the bank just as his father had been, following the death of his own father, the founder. There were changes, too, on the Lloyd side, but the names will only serve to confuse.

A nostalgic moment came in 1845; the lease on the premises at Dale End expired and James Taylor offered the company his family's premises in High Street. These were opened as the headquarters of the bank in 1845. The move cost almost exactly the same amount as it had cost the company to set up nearly ninety years before. Then, in 1852, the firm faced an upheaval of historic proportions. James Taylor, grandson of the original founder, had a mental breakdown. Convinced that he was penniless and that his affairs were in disorder, he took his own life. His name and wealth had been the mainstay of the firm's credit. Indeed, he had over £100,000 in funds outside of the bank as a reserve. A crisis ensued. Taylor's two sons were not interested in banking or the bank and declined offers of a partnership. The Lloyds were left as proprietors. 'We were thus left to bear the responsibility of the bank alone and anxiety could not but be felt lest our credit should not suffice to keep the family together.' They took their chances with the people of Birmingham and in 1853 a new partnership of Lloyds and Company was established. Much the same happened in London, with the Taylor name disappearing from the partnership, the other partner continuing until the take-over of the London company by its country cousin in the 1880s.

The chance that the Lloyds took in Birmingham proved worth while as the business prospered. As Lloyds departed there were new Lloyds to replace them – not always bankers, but trained in the family businesses, usually public figures, councillors and the like. In 1865 when the 'great change' came it was effected by the following partners. They were all descended directly from Sampson Lloyd the Younger, one of the four original partners, Sampson Samuel Lloyd and George B. Lloyd being four generations on through the Farm Lloyds, James and Thomas being only three generations on, as great-grandsons through Charles Lloyd at Bingley.

As a partnership, they were under stiff competition from the joint-stock banks as a result of legislation in 1862 which could limit liability. This added to the attraction of investment in banking and was providing a ready source of new capital by the banks through new share issues. The Lloyds had taken some steps to increase their paid-up capital but there were limits to their disposable wealth. The huge growth of the economy in the nineteenth century meant that banks were being asked to accommodate all kinds of financial arrangements. If liability was limited, the firm's credit would not depend upon individual fortunes. In other words, private banking could no longer do the job of financing the larger enterprises upon which the future of a partnership depended. Attwoods, one of the oldest private banks in Birmingham, failed early in 1865, forcing the Lloyd enterprise to publish its audited accounts and assets to reassure the public. It also had the effect of a prospectus for the step they were to take – the establishment of a joint-stock bank. The private partnership – the second part of the Lloyd story – was at an end.

The new bank opened on 1 May 1865, one hundred years after the first partnership began business. It had been the first private bank and had survived all its competitors. The partners received £50,000 in cash and the same amount in face-value shares. The new issues were immediately over-subscribed, creating a high premium on the shares, and new accounts poured in. The bank was now owned by the public of Birmingham. Its chairman was a man named Kendrick, and Samuel Sampson Lloyd was its first managing director. He was not a Quaker, although, as an act of faith, he purchased back the house at Dolobran for the Lloyds.

So the Lloyd branches stand today in the High Streets of the United Kingdom, their uniform signs ensuring their anonymity, as do those of Barclays. The story of the Lloyd enterprise was not so much that of a bank or an iron-works, but of a family. It was the story of the suffering of Charles in gaol, of the plain and fair dealing of his sons and grandsons, of the banking talents of Charles and George. They were of the eighteenth century but survived well through the nineteenth century. They were contributors and stimulators of the Industrial Revolution and an example of trustworthiness in business and independence of mind. They have been described as being typical examples of the Protestant ethic but no Lloyd ever believed in his predestination to individual power and influence. The members of that family earned that right through honesty, hard work, and social conscience. They gave a bank to a town and their lives in the creation of a city. They obtained no titles but leadership in causes. They stand today as a leading family in the history of the Society of Friends and very much an example of the Quaker success story in business.

CHAPTER 4

The Darbys of Coalbrookdale

Creators of a Revolution

Abraham Darby was an innovative genius whose ideas were fundamental to the creation of an Industrial Revolution. It is scarcely
surprising that the Quakers came to dominate the iron and steel
industry.

He was not the only Friend of genius in iron and steel. There were
many others who received and put their ideas into the mainstream of
Quaker activity in metals, but Abraham Darby stands as in the inventor of two key advances that created the possibility of a shift to mass
production and thereby of a revolution. He was the first of a dynasty of
Quaker ironmasters who over four generations spanned more or less
precisely the rise to power and influence of the Friends in industry
and commerce.

Darby came, like so many Quakers, of yeoman stock. His father,
John Darby, was a smith who lived at Old Farm Lodge, near Dudley, in
what was to become the Black Country.

Although providing a valuable local craft to a rustic community,
John Darby was also a peasant farmer keeping a few beasts and raising
small crops of grain and cutting hay. His son, John Darby II, followed
the same trade but like many an independent yeoman of his time, he
found little in the current style of religion organized round the Establishment to attract him. Repelled by its artificiality and intolerance, he
joined the Society of Friends. Quakerism was to determine the whole
pattern of the life of his family for the next four generations.

His son, Abraham Darby, was born on 14 April 1678. His early life
was spent at a time when the Quakers were generally free of the
repression and persecution that had dogged them. They flocked to the
non-corporate towns that would have them – to Bristol, Warrington,
York, and Birmingham, and to other centres that would become

famous for Quaker enterprise. It was to Birmingham, in fact, that Abraham was sent in the early 1690s as an apprentice to Jonathan Freeth, a master of malt mills. He completed his apprenticeship in 1699, and married Mary Sargant, a member of another family of ironmasters. The couple then went to live in Bristol.

The Friends had always been more than tolerated in Bristol, and several local Quaker enterprises were becoming prominent. Although Abraham initially made his living as a maker of malt mills, it was to brass-working that he turned and in 1702–3 he joined a number of Quaker partners in the setting-up of the famous brass works at Baptist Mills. Possessed of an enquiring nature and keen to explore the possibilities of working in brass and other metals, Abraham visited the Low Countries in 1705 to discover more about working brass and returned with several Dutch families to work at the brass mills.

The following year he acquired a small iron foundry at Cheese Lane in Bristol where he planned to cast iron pots, but his Dutchmen had no success with iron and it was left to another Quaker, Thomas, who had come from the Lloyd forge at Dolobran, to succeed with the casting of bellied iron pots. In 1707 Darby took out a patent process and Thomas signed an undertaking to keep his secrets for a period of three years.

The Severn River was the means of much movement of men and goods between Bristol and East Shropshire. The area around Coalbrookdale was well known to craftsmen and entrepreneurs making their way between these centres, and it was there in the autumn of 1708 that Abraham Darby leased a small, derelict, ironworks. Within a very few months, he was to achieve a breakthrough that would revolutionize the iron industry.

The Severn was a traditional navigation system linking Bristol, the West Midlands and the Border Country. There had always been large numbers of smiths throughout the region plying traditional iron-working crafts. The decline of the South-East as a source of fuel for charcoal burning had led to the construction of mines and works throughout the West Midlands, and particularly in the Black Country. Rod or bar iron, which could be forged and hammered into nails, tools, chains and locks, found its way to the fairs and markets at Dudley and Stourbridge, whence it was distributed to the craftsmen.

By 1700 wrought iron was manufactured in two stages. Iron ore dug from the ground was heated in a blast furnace with a fuel, usually charcoal, and a flux, usually limestone. The furnace would be blown by bellows operated by a water-wheel and normally worked continuously for six to eight months of the year, stopping only in the summer months when water supplies were insufficient to work the bellows.

The temperature would be raised in the furnace and eventually droplets of iron would trickle down from the iron ore into what was called a 'crucible'. This was the lower part of the structure. The limestone would also melt but this would float on the surface of the molten iron. First this slag was drawn off to be discarded as waste and then the iron would be allowed to run out into a mould or channel made in the sand with numerous branches running off at right angles from it. The visual impression of a number of piglets feeding at a sow gave the name of 'pig iron' to the iron produced by this process.

This had then to be taken to forges where it was converted into wrought iron. The pig iron was heated by a charcoal-based process and blown by a blast of air from a water-powered bellows. The iron would melt and as it did so it was stirred with a bar. The oxygen in the air would unite with the carbon in the iron and eventually the pig iron would be converted to a crude form of wrought iron. It was then reheated and hammered. As the rough bar of iron emerged from the hammer it was flattened into a strip between two plain cylindrical rollers powered by a water-wheel. The strip was then moved to the slitting mill where it was passed between rotating discs which would cut it into narrow bars suitable for use by nail-makers and other iron-using craftsmen.

The furnaces where the iron was thus blasted tended to be situated close to the sources of iron ore and to some form of water-power for the bellows. From these blast furnaces pig iron was then distributed over a wider area to the forges. This process of distribution was probably wider than would be imagined. It was known that different proportions of pig iron from different areas would bring about special qualities in wrought iron. Forges in north Shropshire often drew their pig iron not only from nearby furnaces but also from what is now known as Cleveland, the forest of Dean and from Lancashire and Cheshire.

Coalbrookdale lies at the western end of the Severn gorge where the river cuts through the uplands of the east Shropshire coalfield. Since the reign of Queen Elizabeth I mines had been dug in this area because the coal was very close to the surface and could easily be conveyed to customers along the river. By 1700 it was already a busy industrial district. There was an iron furnace making wrought iron in small quantities and during the early years of the seventeenth century Coalbrookdale was becoming the scene of important innovations in iron making by Sir Basil Brooke, Lord of the Manor of Madeley. During the fifty years before Darby set up in Coalbrookdale, Brooke had developed a finery and chafery forge for making pig iron into wrought iron and a steelworks, probably employing a new method of steelmaking which had been introduced into England about 1620.

There was also a large blast furnace dating from 1638. However, some time between 1700 and 1706 water entered the blast furnace as the result of flooding, causing an explosion that rendered it a ruin. The manager, Shadrach Fox, ceased to work it and went to Russia in the service of Peter the Great. Abraham Darby leased this derelict blast furnace in 1708 and his workmen began to reconstruct it. The old hearth was knocked down, new hide bellows were made and by Christmas of 1708 the rehabilitation was complete.

From the start of his operations Abraham Darby used coke as his fuel instead of charcoal and obtained iron of high quality. This was the first time that iron was made successfully using a mineral fuel rather than charcoal. Darby succeeded where others failed because he used coke instead of raw coal and because the coke that he used was largely free of sulphur. The search for an alternative to charcoal had been going on for some time around the country because of the problems of finding wood to make the charcoal. Oak was required for shipbuilding and the development of pine coppices to provide new wood on a twenty-year rotation could not take place at a rate quick enough to keep up with the developing use of iron.

Darby got his unique knowledge of coke during his apprenticeship in the malt trade. He had seen coal coked into cinder as part of a process for drying malt and he may also have developed his acquaintance with the use of coke through his activities in the Bristol brass trade. At all events, from the time the furnace began the accounts show beyond any question that his fuel had come from coal dug from pits and not from charcoal derived from wood.

Darby purchased his iron ore locally from Richard Hartshorne, who had extensive tracts of land for mining which he leased from a variety of landlords. Limestone was purchased from quarries in the area. He began operations with five principal assistants, with the help of day labourers who were hired to carry out various unskilled jobs. Before long workers from Bristol were brought to Coalbrookdale, one of whom was the Quaker John Thomas with whom Darby had entered into an arrangement regarding the making of bellied pots. Patterns for the making of these cast-iron products at Coalbrookdale were imported from Bristol and he began to produce kettles, pots and the bellied cauldrons. In 1710 the works started producing pig iron for forges. Darby experimented with various mixtures of fuels in his blast furnace using coal, charcoal, and even peat.

Coalbrookdale was operating essentially as a foundry but Darby had remained in close touch with the iron trade by investing in the Vale Royal furnace in Cheshire and the Dolgyn iron works near Dolgelley in Merioneth. Three years earlier he had also built a second blast furnace at Coalbrookdale, closer to the River Severn than the original one. It was unusual to have more than one blast furnace in an iron works, but due to the proximity of the river, water power was abundant and whilst it would have been difficult in other circumstances to secure sufficient charcoal to fire two furnaces, the fact that Darby was using coking coal meant that he was able to satisfy the demands of both furnaces.

Darby was an aggressive developer of his business. He had also secured control of the middle and upper forges in Coalbrookdale, the upper forge containing a small finery and shapery works. The lower forge, worked by the Hallen family, was also added to make wrought-iron goods such as handles for the cast-iron wares made by Darby.

When Abraham Darby moved to Coalbrookdale there were no members of the Society of Friends in that area, although there was a meeting house in Broseley not far away. This had been established for some twenty-eight years when he and his family began to attend meetings. Darby himself held office as clerk of the local monthly meeting. This must have involved him in a considerable amount of travel through the Borderland region but we may be sure that such travels were also used by Darby to learn as much as he could about developments in coalmining, and iron working throughout the area. Before long there were eight Quaker families in Darby's parish of Madeley, most of the members of iron-working families living in Coalbrookdale, and by 1717 occasional Quaker meetings were being held in Coalbrookdale itself, although it was not until some time after that a meeting house was erected there.

Darby's first home in Coalbrookdale was at White End, close to the upper forge. By 1712 he had rented Madeley Court, a Tudor mansion about a mile and a half to the east of Coalbrookdale. Soon after 1715 he began constructing a new house on the western side of the dale overlooking the iron-works and it was sufficiently near completion in 1717 for a Quaker meeting to be held there. Abraham attended this meeting although by this time he was very ill. He did not live to occupy the house, for he died on 5 May 1717 and was buried in the Quaker graveyard at Bewdley.

The speed with which Abraham Darby had been able to develop his iron-working interests at Coalbrookdale indicates that at the outset of the enterprise he was no mere ex-apprentice developing a new business. In 1700, fresh from his apprenticeship at the age of twenty, he had been involved in a brass-working business. A small company had been formed, the entire capital of which was subscribed by Bristol merchants. Their undertaking had been favoured by the town's excellent geographical situation for brass working. Coal was mined in the neighbourhood, copper came from Cornwall, the requisite power was provided by the water of the River Frome and the labour problem was solved by bringing in experienced craftsmen from Holland. Another brass company in Bristol, called the Bristol Brass Wire Company, was also run by Quakers and the two ventures must have assisted one another. Business had been profitable, and the Bristol Quakers developed a near monopoly in brass domestic utensils.

It had been Darby's deal with John Thomas over the patent for a new way of casting iron pots and other iron-bellied ware in sand without lowmore clay that had brought about a rift between Darby and his Bristol partners. Darby therefore dissolved his connection with them and presumably it was the money from the dissolution of this partnership that he used to establish the little furnace in Coalbrookdale. There is one other factor which would have contributed to the success of both the brass-works and the iron-works. Much of the iron-working interests of the time were concerned with making shot and cannon for the military. The Quakers have always been pacifists and therefore refused to indulge in this activity; instead they turned themselves to domestic implements which, by the nature of the materials from which they were constructed, were hard wearing and thus much desired by the housewives who had to use them. The Quakers in Bristol and at Coalbrookdale found themselves almost alone in catering for this growing market.

Some finance had to be raised by Abraham Darby in the form of a mortgage on half the property to a Bristol merchant, Thomas Goldney, and this became relevant on his death. His son, also called Abraham, was only six years old when his father died and, in any event, was only entitled to a three-sixteenths share along with his brothers and sisters. Thomas Goldney had a half and another proportion went to Richard Ford, who was the son-in-law of Abraham Darby and his wife, Mary. There were complicated legal wrangles over the succession but Richard Ford and Thomas Goldney were the new masters. They were both Quakers and the books that they kept for the company have survived and provide probably the most complete and meticulous record of any British iron-works of the eighteenth century.

The main trade was in cooking-pots, frying pans, skillets and grates. They were sold to ironmongers throughout the West Midlands and the Borderland and at markets and fairs. They made pig iron at the foundries in Bristol and various other finished products which were sold to a Quaker merchant, Nehemiah Chapman. One aspect of the work at Coalbrookdale at this time was the manufacture of cast-iron parts for steam engines. The first successful steam engine for the pumping of mines had been erected by Thomas Newcomen near Dudley in 1712. By 1719 there was a similar engine at work close to Coalbrookdale. In 1718–19 three cast-iron pipes and a cast box were delivered for a 'fire engine'. Over the next ten years the iron-works at

Coalbrookdale were responsible for casting at least ten cylinders for steam engines. As the demand steadily increased, the works were to supply orders as far afield as Newcastle-on-Tyne, Derbyshire and Flintshire. It was the steam engine more than any other product which brought Coalbrookdale to national prominence.

That was not the end of Coalbrookdale's contribution to the Industrial Revolution. The first iron railway wheels were also cast there during the 1720s. The first railways, made of wood, were constructed on the coalfields to carry coal backwards and forwards. Apparently, the original coalfield to do this was in Shropshire. In 1728 the coalmaster, Richard Hartshorne, built a railway from Little Wenlock to the side of the Severn at Stratshill at Coalbrookdale to carry sand, coal, mines and minerals. In the following year the Coalbrookdale works cast for him eighteen iron railway wheels which, as far as can be discovered, were the first to be used on any railway. In the same year they began to supply other coalmasters with railway wheels and they soon became part of the regular trade of the works.

Abraham Darby II began to take part in the running of the iron works in 1728 when he was seventeen. In 1732 a contract was drawn up recognizing his rights to a quarter of the privileges and advantages of the tenancy of the works, and six years later he was recognized as a full partner. By this time Thomas Goldney had died and his interest in the partnership was now maintained by his son, also called Thomas. Richard Ford died in 1745 after which his three sons retained an interest in the partnership. Abraham Darby II finally purchased these interests in 1756.

The significant development of the 1740s was the introduction of a Newcomen steam engine to the works. One of the problems of a blast furnace is that it has to operate continuously. Once the blast is shut off, various processes have to take place before it can be re-heated. The process of cooling is liable to crack the lining of the furnace. This presented a problem in the eighteenth century because blast furnaces were dependent, in building up heat, on 'blasts of air from bellows', from which they got their name. The bellows were operated by water power. Thus during the summer when the supply of water was extremely variable, it was necessary to shut down the furnaces until the autumn when a supply of water could again be guaranteed. Most iron-works only worked about forty weeks of the year, ceasing operation during the summer when repairs were carried out and raw material was stockpiled.

Traditionally, water had been impounded by constructing a series of pools at various levels, each one feeding down into the next. In 1735 Richard Ford had hit on the idea of pumping the water after it had operated the bellows from the lower pool back to the upper pool, thus lengthening the period when water was available. In 1742–3, the system was improved when Abraham Darby II constructed a steam pumping engine to replace the horse pumps. The engine house was built in December 1742 and January 1743 and the engine was finally set to work the following summer. The first Abraham Darby had been acquainted with the Newcomen steam engine, yet this was the first time that a steam engine had been applied to the making of iron. By maintaining a circuit of water between the pools the engine made it no longer necessary to cease work in the summer.

For the second time in the two generations, the Darbys of Coalbrookdale had furnished the iron industry with an innovation that was to revolutionize iron production. The introduction of the steam pump was to provide one of the principal foundations for the iron industry during the Industrial Revolution.

Although the making and selling of castings had been profitable, it was the manufacture of wrought iron that was essentially the mainstream of the iron trade. The use of coke as the fuel in his blast meant difficulties in creating pig iron that was suitable for use by the forge masters. Like Crosfield, who experimented in chemicals, and Cadbury, who experimented with mortar and pestle to obtain new constituents for cocoa, George Palmer endlessly trying out new processes to produce biscuits, and Benjamin Huntsman working on steel processes, Darby was determined to solve the problem of creating pig iron from a coke blast furnace, and he experimented throughout the 1740s. An account of that period preserves the tradition that Darby spent six days and nights without sleep at the furnace until he finally produced iron of the desired quality. Tradition has it that he had to be carried home asleep by his workmen. One of the secrets of his final success was the careful selection of grades of iron ore with a low phosphorus content. But the new process involved something more than the mere choice of raw material; Abraham Darby II had that particular skill of the Quakers as an applied scientist, in being able to turn theoretical concepts to practical applications. His results were so successful that by the early 1750s he was erecting new furnaces to cater for the demand for the pig iron that he produced.

The Darbys of Coalbrookdale had made a significant contribution to the use of power in iron manufacture, and the development of raw material. One of their other great achievements in the 1740s lay in the development of communications. Railways were used in the Coalbrookdale area to carry coal from the mines to the banks of the Severn, and in 1749 the first major railway line to suply an iron-works was built. This was a railway from Coalmoor to the Coalbrookdale works, for the purpose of carrying coal, ironstone and other materials for the use of the iron-works. It was the first of many railway lines that the

Coalbrookdale partners were to build during the next hundred years.

During the 1740s Abraham Darby II established himself as a senior partner at the Coalbrookdale works. One of the instincts of many of the Quaker entrepreneurs was the establishment of horizontal integration, controlled by themselves in their industry. This was very true of the iron industry; the Lloyd family came to control virtually every aspect of iron production and distribution in the Birmingham area. In 1740 the Coalbrookdale partners had done no more than operate the furnaces and cast iron products. They had purchased their raw materials from local coalmasters or landowners.

In the 1750s Abraham Darby began to lease mining rights over large tracts of land and started a process of integration which made the Shropshire iron-works one of the largest industrial enterprises in Great Britain. In March 1754 Darby leased the mines in the township of Great Dawley from the Slaney family. At about the same time he leased mines in the Manor of Ketley from Earl Gower and began to build a steam engine to drain them. He purchased Horsehay Farm from the Slaneys which contained an old water corn-mill and its pools. Darby and his workmen transformed the whole landscape of the area around Horsehay Park. They built a new dam in order to take the enlarged pool. The construction of a furnace with its attendant buildings was begun in the summer of 1754, and new railways were laid to serve the works, linking it with Coalbrookdale and the Severn, with coal and iron mines in Dawley and with limestone quarries in Little Wenlock. A steam engine to recycle the water to the pool was supplied from Coalbrookdale. The Horsehay Farm site was close to their newly leased mine, and Darby and the younger Goldney spent much time and money creating it as the focal point of their production interests.

Quakers were always concerned with the intelligent siting of their businesses. The first load of iron ore from the pits arrived on 1 May 1755. Two weeks later the furnace was making iron and before long was making on average between fifteen and twenty-two tons. It was the first time that a coke-fired furnace has been proved conclusively superior to one fired with charcoal and almost all the pig iron produced was sold to forge masters. Much of it went to the Knight and Foley families who controlled the most important iron-forging partnership in the West Midlands.

The Seven Years' War, bringing with it a demand for munitions, together with restrictions on the importing of foreign iron, greatly increased the price of iron in England. In April 1756 Darby and Goldney agreed to erect another furnace at Horsehay and in October of that year they leased fourteen acres of land in the Manor of Ketley for the construction of two further furnaces. A series of pools was constructed in the Valley of the Ketley Brook and a steam engine was supplied to recirculate water.

In 1759 Darby leased a large tract of land, the Newdale Estate, on the borders of Dawley and Wellington parishes. His first intention may have been to build a new foundry but in the end the area was used entirely for mining. Other partnerships were also moving into the district, including the New Willey Company of which the famous John Wilkinson was a partner. The name Wilkinson lives on today as a brand name for metal products.

In all, nine blast furnaces were built within four miles of Coal-brookdale in the four years between 1755 and 1758. It was to establish Coalbrookdale as the most important iron-making district in Great Britain. The death of the second Abraham Darby at the age of fifty-one in 1763 accords with the end of this expansion.

In the first half century, the Darby enterprise made a unique contribution to the history of an industry that was vital to the Industrial Revolution. Abraham Darby had developed a process using mineral fuel which was in abundant supply instead of charcoal which was not. His son had developed his father's innovations although he was a man who gave practical application to ideas rather than being an inventor himself. His genius was to put together a package of ideas and make from them something more than the mere sum of their parts. By experiment he found out how to make forge pig iron using coke. He applied his knowlege of the workings of steam engines to the problem of recycling water from the furnace pools. He looked at the existing uses of the Shropshire railways and re-adapted them in the service of his iron-works. He understood the basic problem of securing reliable supplies of raw materials. He knew that it was necessary for iron-masters to lease the mines and organize their operation themselves. Lastly, he was to synthesize all these ideas at model centres like Horsehay and Ketley. He sank pits and installed steam engines to keep them dry; from the pits ore and coal was taken by his railways to his furnaces, where the ore was reduced to pig iron which in turn was taken by his own railways to the Severn, along which barges took it to his customers.

When Abraham Darby II died, there was again a break in the Darby control of the Coalbrookdale works. His son, the third Abraham, was aged only eleven and the management of Coalbrookdale was taken over by Abraham Darby's son-in-law, Richard Reynolds. The Reynolds were a well-known Bristol Quaker family who had moved to Shropshire in 1756. They represented the interests of the Goldneys in the iron-works. Reynolds had married the second Abraham Darby's daughter, Hannah, and had established a home at Ketley Bank House. The name Reynolds itself was to become famous amongst eighteenth-century iron-masters through his son William who was a grandson of Abraham Darby. Whether credit should be given to the Darbys or the Reynolds for this is a matter of debate.

Richard Reynolds proved to be an able manager of the business and several important developments in the affairs of Coalbrookdale took place under his direction in the 1760s. He re-negotiated the mining leases with Earl Gower in 1764. The mines at Donnington Wood and Wrockwardine Wood were particularly important as sources of iron ore for the Ketley and Horsehay furnaces. As a local man Reynolds was keenly aware of that fact. In 1767 he used iron rails for the first time. For some time two level wooden rails had been employed with the advantage that when the top section was worn out by the traffic it could be replaced without disturbing the track. Reynolds's first iron rails were simply thin strips of cast iron about 6 ft by 3½ in which replaced the top levels of the wooden rails. Iron rails were then applied to many of the partnership's routes. In 1768 they began to produce these rails at Horsehay in considerable number and were thus able not only to supply their own needs but the demands of others as well.

Reynolds seems to have possessed the usual Quaker interest in technological developments. He was involved in the attempt made by George and Thomas Cranedge to make wrought iron from pig iron in a reverberatory furnace, using the Darby coke-based process. These experiments were carried out in Coalbrookdale and the brothers took out a patent in 1766, but the experiment proved wasteful and it was abandoned. The idea eventually became synthesized in a later process patented in 1784. The major technological developments of the time did not happen out of the blue; they grew out of a continuing series of experiments, of trial and error, carried out all over the country. Reynolds was as concerned with innovation as his wife's grandfather Abraham Darby. He performed a valuable role as Goldney had before him in seeing the firm safely through a period of transition between the managements of successive generations of Darbys.

The third Abraham Darby entered the works in 1768 at the age of eighteen and was followed a few years later by his younger brother, Samuel. At this time the Darbys had three major iron-works. There were two blast furnaces at Coalbrookdale and at Horsehay and three at Ketley, and they had forges for turning pig iron into wrought iron at Coalbrookdale and Bridgenorth. They held leases on various tracts of mining land extending from Donnington in the north of Shropshire to the River Severn, and also owned warehouses in various parts of England and civil tracts of farmland in Madeley.

Liverpool was another great nonconformist provincial town at this time which, like Bristol, had prospered as a west-facing port on the one hand, with the proximity of sources of raw materials and power on the other. Like Bristol, Birmingham and York, Liverpool was a great centre for Quakerism and had its share of substantial Quaker family enterprises. Not the least of these were those of the Rathbone family and it was during the time of Abraham Darby III that we find the two families coming together in their business interests. The direct connection with Abraham Darby was through his interests in merchant ships, trading from Liverpool.

Three years after joining the company, at the age of twenty-one, Abraham Darby took a quarter interest in the ship *Darby* which was sailing from Liverpool to Danzig and returning with cargoes of timber. His sister had married Joseph Rathbone in the year that he had entered the Darby business. The connection was further reinforced some twenty years later when William Reynolds's sister, granddaughter of the second Darby, also married a Rathbone. At all events Abraham Darby III remitted his share of the capital in the ship *Darby* through Joseph Rathbone. The connection between the two families grew and over the next thirty years the interests of the Darbys, the Reynolds and the Rathbones were closely intermixed, operating to the individual benefit of each family.

Throughout the 1770s and early 1780s the Coalbrookdale concern shared in full the prosperity of the Shropshire iron industry. The new Darby in the company continued the aggressive expansion of his father and grandfather into new plant. In 1776 he purchased blast furnaces on the banks of the Severn. The firm also took over the local Madeley Field coalworks, and built another major iron-works at Donnington Wood where two furnaces were erected between 1783 and 1785 close to the mines on land that they had leased from Earl Gower.

Not content simply with turning out pig iron Darby went ahead and enlarged the Coalbrookdale forges which would turn the pig iron into wrought iron. Water-wheels were constructed to turn new slitting mills at Coalbrookdale in 1776 and in the early 1780s a new forge was constructed at Horsehay, initially water powered, but later worked by steam engine. This forge specialized in producing plates for the manufacture of boilers. A new steam power forge was also introduced at Ketley in 1785.

Abraham Darby III continued the family interest in the development of power-assisted machinery. His interests were twofold. First of all, the machinery itself represented an important use of his iron, and secondly, because the machines themselves were being developed for a wide variety of manufacturing purposes involving iron. Thus it was good commercial business as well as their inbred technical curiosity that kept the partners closely in contact with new developments in the steam engine.

The Coalbrookdale partners were closely connected at this time with James Watt and Mathew Boulton whose first improved steam engines were developed in 1776. One was in operation close by at John Wilkinson's works and its success encouraged them to install Boulton and Watt machines at their Ketley iron-works between 1778 and 1780. Furthermore, in 1781, the old Newcomen pumping engine that had revolutionized that aspect of iron-work at Coalbrookdale was itself replaced by a large Boulton and Watt engine named the 'Resolution'. They went on to install many new engines to the designs of James Watt during the following decade. In many ways the years of Abraham Darby III can be identified as the high point of Coalbrookdale. The business was so soundly established that they were able to indulge in the Darbys' instinct for aggressive expansion. They continued to lease new tracts of mining land and develop warehousing interests in distant parts of the country, going on to take an interest in limestone mining and quarrying as limestone was an essential raw material for iron making. During the time of Abraham Darby III, Coalbrookdale was the centre of the largest single iron-making concern in Great Britain.

Abraham Darby III also had an interest in acquiring farmland. Quakers in other businesses often acquired agricultural property, but these were usually town-based entrepreneurs of a hundred years later who sought agricultural property as a means of obtaining credentials for entering Parliament. Abraham Darby's interest, though he had yeoman forebears, was severely practical. Working farms offered numerous advantages for ironmasters. They needed large numbers of horses for the operation of the railways. The establishment of Ketley as a focal point for an integrated iron concern had meant the construction of railways to link their various interests. The laying of railway lines at that time would have posed exactly the same problem as the construction of roads and rail links today, in terms of landowners, permissions and compensation. The ownership of farmland would facilitate the building of a new railway by making it easier to obtain the necessary rights of way.

Food riots amongst workers were not uncommon in the second half of the 1700s. Ownership of a farm meant that the iron-masters were to some extent able to control the supply of food to their workers. Abraham Darby III worked no less than three farms. The first, Sunnyside Farm, seems to have been used largely to supply horses for the works. These were obtained from fairs such as that held at Lichfield, and were supplied in teams to take goods in waggons from the iron-works to such places as Chester and Bedworth. The Hay Farm was operated more conventionally, and apparently Darby spent money on its improvement during the 1770s. Many fruit trees were planted and new cattle acquired. By 1776 Darby's income from the farms included the sale of wheat, barley, sheep and horses. As with other successful Quaker businessmen the various facets of his life were closely connected.

The most famous monument of all to the Darbys of Coalbrookdale is the Iron Bridge. The building of the first bridge of iron was something which captured the imagination of Darby's contemporaries, and it stands to this day. From 1500 onwards there was a population of miners, potters, boat builders, bargemen and, later, iron-workers along the banks of the river. As there was no bridge in the gorge, passengers were carried over the river by various ferries which were not reliable and could even be dangerous. Heavy commodities like iron ore and limestone had to be carried by barges.

There had been various proposals to construct a bridge between Madeley and Broseley or Benthall. It was a difficult project: the banks were steep, adequate approaches were difficult and there was a high density of shipping from the Severn. However, in September 1775 a group of interested people met in Broseley, deciding on the best site for a bridge, its northern end being in what was called Madeley Wood. Thomas Pritchard, an architect, was instructed to prepare a design. Abraham Darby III did not attend the meeting, but was appointed Treasurer to the project, he and his brother Samuel being the only members of the Coalbrookdale partnership to be involved with the bridge scheme at the outset.

In October 1775 Pritchard completed his plan for an iron bridge, four ribs spanning 120 ft. He worked out with Abraham Darby that the cost of the structure would be some £3,200. It was some time before work began but in November 1777, after the death of Thomas Pritchard, regular work began on the project. Accounts suggest that during the following year between twenty and thirty men were working on the bridge at any one time, augmented by groups of labourers brought in for short spells. During 1778 the high stone abutments were constructed. Work ceased during the winter months when the river was high, but in March 1779 it seems that Darby's workmen were preparing to erect the iron-work. By the end of the month most of the parts were laid on the bank ready for construction. A barge was hired and on 1 and 2 July the first pair of ribs was hauled into place. The completion of the main structure went ahead quite quickly and there was a celebration on 23 October to mark that event, but it was not until New Year's Day, 1781 that the bridge was finally opened to traffic. The delay was due mainly to slowness in the construction of access roads, particularly on the north bank. The final cost of erecting the bridge was £2,737 4s 4d. The bridge contains nearly 400 tons of castings which would have kept Darby's blast furnace busy for three or four months. Although a great achievement the bridge was an extremely costly one. It remained unique for quite some time; it gained Abraham Darby the gold medal of the Society of Arts, and he was presented with a model of the bridge in mahogany.

The construction of the bridge had an enormous effect on the future planning and construction of roads in the area. The influence of enlightened self-interest can again be seen in the affairs of the Darbys. The construction of the bridge meant that a road system would not only bring traffic onto his land but would also service his own interests. Abraham Darby was already concerned with the road system. He and his brother Samuel were the trustees of the Wenlock Turnpike Trust which was responsible for a network of roads radiating from the town of Much Wenlock. Darby's accounts show that he sent £20 to the trust in 1779 towards the cost of obtaining the Act of Parliament necessary for the renewal of its powers. Abraham and Samuel were also trustees of the road that ran from Turnbridge to Coalbrookdale which gave direct access from the country town of Shrewsbury to the iron bridge. When this road was formally opened to traffic in 1779 many of its first users were sightseers going to look at the half-completed bridge. Each user was required to pay a toll on this turnpike.

The building of the Shropshire canal was another major development in the 1780s, the first local canal to be authorized by an Act of Parliament. The system dated from the mid-1760s when Earl Gower had built the Donnington Wood canal on his estate. Needless to say, the Donnington Wood land was leased by Abraham Darby. This was a private waterway on private land. In 1788 an Act was obtained for the Shropshire canal to extend from Donnington Wood to Southall Bank from where there were to be two lines to the Severn. One line went to Coalbrookdale and the other to Hay Farm. At both ends of this new navigation was land belonging to Abraham Darby.

At the point where in Hay Farm the canal joined the Severn, there grew up a new town of Coalport with its wharves, china factories, chain works and rows of cottages. Abraham Darby had sold the site where Coalport was built to the Reynolds family shortly before the construction of the canal began. Although Abraham Darby was not a shareholder in the Shropshire canal, his brother Samuel was not only one of the initial subscribers but also a treasurer of the concern. The genius behind the Shropshire canal system may not have been Abraham Darby himself but it was certainly his cousin William Reynolds. He surveyed the route and supervised its construction.

Abraham Darby III was active throughout his life in the affairs of the Society of Friends. The money collected at various Quaker meetings was carefully recorded in his account book. Regular meetings were held at Coalbrookdale and Darby left provision for the maintenance of the meeting-house and graveyard in his will.

He died in 1789 at the relatively early age of thirty-nine. By that time Coalbrookdale had become the most celebrated industrial region in Great Britain. Engineers and manufacturers from all over Europe flocked there to examine the new techniques in iron-making and transportation for which it was famous. Journalists, writers, artists and sightseers were attracted by the extraordinary landscape of pit-heads, waste tips and blazing furnaces. Few of the innovations of the Industrial Revolution which involved the use of iron have no connection with the Coalbrookdale area. The connections with Boulton and Watt, the pioneers of the steam engine, with John Wilkinson, the other local ironmaster, Lord Dundonald the pioneer of the distillation of coal tar and alkali manufacture, William Jessop, the eminent canal engineer of the time, John Macadam, the greatest road builder of his time, and Thomas Telford – all ensured that Coalbrookdale became the focal point of intellectual and practical intercommunication in the applied sciences that created the Industrial Revolution for Britain. It is impossible to over-estimate the contribution of Abraham Darby III, his father and grandfather, to the social history of this country.

It is a curious paradox that on each occasion when a member of the Darby dynasty died, the youngsters of the next generation were not quite old enough to take over the business and an interregnum became necessary. For the third time this occurred when Abraham Darby III died, his eldest son, Francis, being only six years old. Abraham's brother Samuel died at the age of forty-one in 1796. His son, Edmund, was by that time only fourteen.

The complex pattern of the Darby, Reynolds and Rathbone partnership made progress for the enterprise difficult. Large parts of the Darby family's assets were mortgaged to Richard Reynolds or to the Rathbones. Apparently during the ten years after Abraham Darby III's death, the quality of the production and distribution services offered by the partnership suffered. There was clearly a lack of strong overall direction to the company and eventually in July 1796 the interests of the Darby and Reynolds families in the associated works in Shropshire were separated. The Reynolds took full control of the Ketley and Madeley Wood iron-works and their associated mines. The Darbys took Coalbrookdale and Horsehay, retaining for themselves the right to trade as the Coalbrookdale Company. The blast furnaces at Donnington Wood were sold off in 1796, and various other small concerns were either taken over by individual members of the companies or were sold. The controlling shareholders of the Coalbrookdale Company were now the surviving daughters of Abraham Darby II, i.e. the sisters of Samuel and Abraham III, as well as their widows, Deborah and Rebecca.

From 1803 a member of the Darby family, Edmund, who was Samuel's son, was again in charge of the works, and once again it moved to the forefront of technological progress. The success of the iron bridge led ultimately to bridge-building becoming one of the major concerns of the company. This took some time to happen, for over a decade after its completion the iron bridge remained a curiosity. In the 1790s, however, various attempts were made to copy it. The great flood on the Severn in February 1795 severely damaged every bridge over the river except the iron bridge, which braved the storm. Almost immediately Coalbrookdale began to supply castings for other iron bridges. They produced iron-work for Thomas Telford and for other bridges in Shrewsbury and Somerset, and also for John Nash's second bridge in 1797 at Stanford in Worcester. A succession of other bridges followed, including two for the Bristol Box Company and a fifty-ton bridge exported to Jamaica in 1807.

They continued their interests in the steam-engine business and many such engines were manufactured at Coalbrookdale in the 1780s. They maintained their connection with James Watt and built a number of engines under licence to him, but at the same time they also worked to designs by other engineers such as Adam Heslop and James Sadler. Of all the engineers associated with the company at this time, Richard Trevithick was the most outstanding. He was possessed of an innovatory turn of mind and contributed as much to the development of steam power as Watt himself. Richard went to Coalbrookdale in 1796 and within four years had built a high-pressure engine as an experiment.

Before the end of the same year he constructed the first steam railway locomotive to run on the Coalbrookdale plate ways, and between 1800 and 1810 the works supplied several of his engines. During this period Coalbrookdale became a leading supplier of steam engines, ranging from the now routine Boulton and Watt machines, the more traditional Newcomen atmospheric engines, to the advanced Trevithick engines.

The excursion by the Darbys into civil engineering was not to cease with the construction of bridges. In addition to providing iron for machines and other manufacturing processes, they went into the architectural use of cast iron. Attingham Park, built for the first Lord Berwick in 1784 and enlarged by John Nash in 1805, contained a glass-and-iron roof in the picture gallery. The range of products that poured out of Coalbrookdale at the beginning of the nineteenth century was extremely varied, and included cast stamp heads for the dressing plants at Cornish tin mines, anvil blocks, powder mill beds, lathe frames and sugar rolls. For agriculture they made ploughs, milk pans, and presses, for the domestic consumer they produced bedsteads, bookcases, clock weights, kettles, frying-pans, shoe-scrapers and a variety of grids, stones and ovens.

The products of the Horsehay works were less varied. Most of the pig iron from the furnaces went to forges in North Worcestershire and South Staffordshire and a considerable amount went to the forges at Horsehay, itself to be ultimately sold as wrought iron. They also produced wrought-iron boilers which were sold to steam-engine users throughout the Midlands.

During the first decade of the nineteenth century – the period of the Napoleonic Wars – the firm shared in the general prosperity of the industry, although there is no record of their having being involved in the manufacture of armaments. It is difficult to imagine how there would have been any room for such a specialization. The wartime boom came to an end and after the peace of 1815 prices sank and Coalbrookdale faced many difficulties. There was increasing competition coming from South Wales and the Black Country. The Coalbrookdale blast furnaces were both old and relatively remote from productive mines, which involved high transport costs. The works was run upon old plans of forty years previously, and the basic inefficiency which was hidden during a period of higher turnover now could be seen. The Coalbrookdale blast furnaces were finally blown out about 1818 and henceforth Coalbrookdale was simply a foundry making castings from pig iron and smelted elsewhere. The forges were to cease production some twenty-four years later. Yet even during this period Coalbrookdale had its achievements. In 1816 the parts for the foot-bridge over the Liffey at Dublin were cast at Coalbrookdale and in the following year a 120-ft cast-iron bridge to cross the Irwell between Salford and Strangeways was completed. In 1820 the company provided the massive iron columns which support the brick arches of the Macclesfield bridge over the Regent's Canal to the north of Regent's Park. The bridge is there to be seen to this day by people taking the boat trip from Camden Town to the Grand Union Canal in Paddington.

Edmund Darby died in 1810, by which time Francis Darby, the son of the third Abraham, was ready to take over the management of the iron-works. He did so in association with Barnard Dickinson who was the husband of his sister Anne. A fourth Abraham Darby was to join the firm in the late 1820s along with his brother Alfred. They were sons of Edmund and were ultimately to take over responsibility for the management of Horsehay. Little can be said of the period between 1810 and 1830 under Edmund Darby's management, and it wasn't until another Abraham took over that the business prospered again.

After 1830 Abraham and Alfred Darby, sons of Edmund, embarked on an ambitious programme of reforms. They insisted that the boilers which provided the steam for the large steam engines at the iron-works should be fired by slack instead of high-quality coke. This not only reduced operating costs, saving between six and seven hundred tons of coal a month, but apparently it also led to a general improvement in the local environment. The two brothers were constantly present on the premises. Any waste products of the works which had an iron content were introduced into the furnaces to raise the output. They built a new blast furnace in 1834 and in 1838 the furnaces at Horsehay were converted to operate with Neilson's hot-blast system.

Alterations were also carried out at the forges. There are many technical expressions associated with iron processing not least that known rather charmingly as 'puddling'. One system of puddling introduced by Joseph Hall, known as 'pig boiling', was introduced in 1832 at the works and soon after guide mills were installed. There were new steam engines to drive hammers and mills, and one way and another the complex at Coalbrookdale was vigorously rationalized and a skilled labour force built up. In twenty years it was redeveloped to become possibly the largest foundry in the world. Two new blast furnaces had been opened at Dawley Castle some time before. These furnaces were rebuilt with a new blowing engine designed by Samuel Cookson of Coalbrookdale and a hot blast was introduced in 1839. In the same year the company purchased another iron-works between Horsehay and Coalbrookdale which added more blast furnaces to the Darbys' concern. To this was added the Lawley furnace, formerly the property of the Ketley company which lay on the Darbys' mining territory. The Darbys' works were linked together by railways and some time after 1820 a new route was constructed down the Lightmoor Valley to Coalbrookdale along which all the products of Horsehay, Lightmoor, Dawley Castle and Lawley, together with coal and other materials, could pass the Severn side wharves.

The fourth generation of Darbys extended the company's interests in iron-making to other parts of the country, purchasing the works at Ebbw Vale in 1844, as well as works on the South Wales coalfield at Abersychn, Abercarn and Pontypool. Although Coalbrookdale's contribution to the national economy was now smaller, it remained a very important iron making business, excelling at this time in its castings which were of an extremely high quality, and in high-grade wrought-iron boiler plates. In 1838 two plates measuring 10ft 7in by 5ft 1in were displayed at Liverpool and were claimed to be the largest ever rolled. The plates for the S.S. *Great Britain* were also rolled by the company in the early 1840s.

The brothers were fortunate in having the Great Exhibition at the Crystal Palace in 1851 to act as a stimulus. It brought more fame to the company than any other event since the completion of the iron bridge. At the entrance to the northern end of the Crystal Palace stood an impressive range of ornamental gates, 60ft wide, cast at Coalbrookdale.

There was also a towering cast-iron dome 30ft high supported on six pillars, each of which was surmounted by a falcon. There was also a figure of an eagle slayer with his bow and the slain eagle pinned to the roof by the arrow which had transfixed it. The company also exhibited an ornamental fountain, 'The Boy and The Swan', a cast-iron altar rail and various items of garden furniture. They were fortunate in being able to employ the services of John Bell, one of the most fashionable designers of his time. The commissioners for the exhibition invited Abraham Darby IV in January 1852 to re-erect the ceremonial gates at the entrance to Kensington Gardens. They can be seen today at the entrance to Kensington Gardens not far from the Albert Hall. Despite the company's work in ornamental cast-iron work, the traditional aspects of work at Coalbrookdale continued, with pots, pans, kettles and other forms of domestic hardware.

From the middle of the nineteenth century the connection of the Darby family with the iron-works gradually diminished. Abraham and Alfred were members of the fifth generation of Darbys to manage the Coalbrookdale iron works and by this time, as so many other families of successful industrialists had done, they began to take an interest in landed estates. By 1851 Abraham had a home at Stokeport near Slough, and Alfred acquired a Jacobean mansion at Stanley Hall near Bridgenorth. As their involvement diminished there was a substantial contraction of the activities of the Coalbrookdale company. In the early 1860s the blast furnaces at Horsehay were blown out and in 1883 the company ceased to smelt iron altogether when the furnaces at Whitemoor and Dawley Castle ceased production. This was common, for nearly all the furnaces in Shropshire ceased to work at this time. The high cost of raw material made it almost impossible to compete with iron-works near to the coast. By 1900 the Coalbrookdale company's principal concerns were its brickworks – a side-line in 1850 – and the foundry at Coalbrookdale itself. The brothers had left the day-to-day direction of affairs at the Shropshire iron-works of the Coalbrookdale company in the hands of managers. In 1881 the Coalbrookdale company went the way of many Quaker enterprises by being organized as a public limited liability company. Alfred Darby II served as its chairman from 1886 until 1925. When he retired he brought the direct link between the Darbys and the iron-works to an end, although two members of the family are still connected with the Ironbridge Gorge Museum Trust which administers the site of an old furnace and the works museum at Coalbrookdale.

CHAPTER 5

The Crosfields of Warrington

Crosfield is not today a household name. The family enterprise was located in Warrington, and the efforts of Joseph Crosfield are no less significant than those of the other Quakers. The name of Crosfield was absorbed earlier this century, first into Lever Brothers and finally into the mighty Unilever combine. It is a testament to the Crosfield enterprise that their venture remains a significant part of Unilevers and, unlike many companies, has survived the inevitable rationalizations of the conglomerate.

The Crosfields came from Cumberland. George Fox had found that the far North-West was fertile ground for his freethinking ideas. Far removed from the Court, the archbishops, and usually the army, the locals were less than interested in the values of the London Establishment. There was little to challenge the view of the north-western man of substance that he was lord and master of his own plot – free to act and think as he saw fit. Such attitudes meant greater freedom for lesser beings to make their own way towards God, truth and understanding, and it was among the many groups of 'seekers after truth' that Fox found support for his ideas.

The Crosfields were amongst the earliest supporters of Fox. After the Restoration and the re-establishment of the Church, they refused to pay church tithes and met with the usual distraint of their goods. Despite this they prospered as yeomen farmers and George Crosfield was to find himself farming seventy-seven acres at Low Park, End Moor. He married Jane Rowlandson, a remarkable woman who travelled in the ministry throughout the British Isles and the New World.

George, their son, was sent to be apprenticed to a relative in Kendal who ran a grocery business. The Quakers were always insistent that their sons should receive an appropriate preparation for their lives at work and even the sons of wealthy Quakers would be twenty-one or twenty-two before they earned any wages. Young George Crosfield completed his apprenticeship and moved to Warrington where he purchased a minority interest in a business that combined grocery with importing tea. He eventually acquired the business and with good training and practical experience behind him proceeded to run it. He was a typical Quaker, a man of an exact mind, methodical and persevering. Even as an apprentice in Kendal he kept careful accounts.

He could be seen, even on a cold winter's day, patiently riding a horse to Liverpool to purchase his goods. He would stay with friends whilst he supervised the loading of his stores and tea onto a small boat which would then leave for the journey up river to Warrington.

He married a Warrington girl and, like a good Quaker, sired thirteen children. Like his father, he refused to pay church tithes and local records show that his goods were distrained for the privilege. This lack of respect for the Anglican Church did not prevent him from attaining considerable status locally. His industry, plain dealing and practical business sense meant that the grocery business prospered and gave him standing as a man of substance, qualities which also endeared him to others at a personal level, for he was often called upon to arbitrate in local disputes and to execute wills. He was a great supporter of the town's circulating library.

He moved to Lancaster in 1799 to manage a new venture, a sugar refinery, in association with merchant associates from Liverpool. Imagine his disappointment one year later when the refinery was burnt to the ground. George rebuilt the refinery over the next twenty years. Three of his sons had been left to manage the business in Warrington, the fourth, Joseph, being sent as apprentice to Newcastle on Tyne. Young Joseph was to learn the trade of chemist and druggist from another Quaker, Anthony Clapham. Tyneside was very much a centre for the growing chemical industry with its incursions into glass-making and soap-boiling.

To the practical business skills Joseph Crosfield added a sound technical knowledge of chemical processes. Clapham was developing one of the biggest soapworks at Newcastle and it was both the management of the works, as well as the technical processes of a soapery, that caught Joseph's interest.

He completed his apprenticeship in 1813 when he was twenty-one, and journeyed to see his father in Lancaster. He was anxious to get into the soapmaking business on his own account. He wanted his father's opinion: would he favour such a move? More important, would he help him with capital to start the enterprise? George Crosfield was in favour but it was not until the following year that he went to Warrington to view some premises near the river that might be suitable for a soapery. He gave his consent and Joseph completed the purchase of the site and premises. After another short visit to Newcastle, Joseph began the business of making soap at Bank's Quay in Warrington.

Joseph had chosen well, both in terms of his business and its site. The soapery was part of the new industry growing in the area. Merseyside was becoming an important centre for chemical, soap and glass manufacture. The emergent Lancashire cotton industry demanded soap for bleaching, dyeing and calico printing. Elsewhere demand was growing for other by-products of soapmaking, such as soda. Joseph had his raw materials to hand in the salt fields of Cheshire and his fuel at the St Helens and Wigan coalfaces. The Mersey had recently been linked through the new canal systems to Birmingham, Bristol, Nottingham and London.

Warrington stood at the lowest bridging point of the Mersey. It was also a major crossroads on the western route to Scotland and the route from Liverpool to Manchester. Most important, vessels up to 100 tons unloaded their cargoes at Bank's Quay, the very site of Joseph's soap works. George Crosfield had given his son £1,500 to buy the premises and start the business. Every penny of this was lost in the first year – as times were against him, and he survived only by leasing part of the premises to a Quaker corn merchant who allowed him the combined use of the mill to grind kelp. This was to cause further problems for Joseph a couple of years later when Thomas Tipping, the corn merchant, found himself in debt for £14,000. Joseph was owed some £800.

The Quakers were very careful to keep an eye on the business affairs of members of the Society. If irregularities occurred, debts unpaid or credit over-extended, then a small group of Friends would analyse the books of the enterprise and advise the members on the best course of action. Tipping's goods were put up for sale. Since some of the money due was Joseph's, he decided to buy the corn mills' machinery, using the rest of the soapery as security in order to raise a loan to purchase Tipping's equipment. Having obtained a corn business he then leased it to Messrs. William and Thomas Wagstaffe.

In the same year, 1815, Joseph's father died leaving a legacy of £1,500. Quakers were naturally close as family people and his father's death would have weighed heavily on Joseph at a critical time in his own business career. One move he did make was to take his cousin Joseph Fell as a financial partner.

Trade generally began to improve, and more workers were being employed in the smoky towns of industrial England and were enjoying a higher standard of living. Demand for soap increased correspondingly. Cleanliness was an alternative to godliness in Victorian

England, for in the next twenty years consumption per head of soap increased from 3lb to 7lb per annum. As the nation grew cleaner, Crosfields grew, and by 1835 they were producing nearly 1,000 tons of soap per annum. This placed the Company in the top ten per cent of the three hundred odd soap manufacturers in the country.

Joseph had over this time established a successful and solid enterprise, although for the next seventeen years he only made minimal additions to the capital value of the Company in the form of additions or improvements. He preferred to spread his money around. Today the spirit of venture capitalism survives only in a limited form – the concept of continually backing speculative ventures is not something that appeals to contemporary financiers who have largely replaced the nineteenth-century type of entrepreneur. Joseph lived in an age of enormous technical expansion where endless speculative projects were devised and supported. Instead of re-investing his profits for expansion and improvement, he diversified. Between 1826 and 1845 Joseph received over £25,000 in profits, but his holding was rarely above £12,000 in value. This was to backfire on him because his partner Fell did re-invest his share of the profits. When Fell died in 1834 Joseph was required to pay substantial sums to Fell's executors to obtain the rights to the whole business. It should be said that Joseph Crosfield's losses were invariably small. Many of his investments were in projects that ultimately proved successful and profitable, though not until after his death.

He is described by his contemporaries as a great and good man, full of kindness, scattering goods where they were most needed. The *Warrington Guardian* described him as 'one of the most able public men the town had ever had'. Given his status as a successful businessman, such eulogy might be taken for granted except for one important factor. The *Guardian* was Conservative, owned by Tory interests and committed to the interests of the Establishment, and Joseph Crosfield was radical, anti-Establishment and a member of the Liberal Party. Joseph campaigned for the great radical measures of his day – the repeal of the Test and Corporation Acts, Parliamentary reform, free trade and on behalf of the Anti-Corn Law League.

As a Quaker entrepreneur Joseph was typical of his kind. His nonconformist, provincially-based religious ideology may partly explain his radical politics, but a greater determinant lay in the fact that the successful entrepreneurs that grew out of the Industrial Revolution were a new breed that had little in common with the traditional Tory landowners. Their success lay within their local community – they were aware of the roots of their success and the importance of progressive reform to improve the quality of life for their workers.

Joseph Crosfield shared the traditional Quaker regard for education and apart from the Quaker School, he was concerned with the establishment of the Warrington Educational Society and the Warrington Mechanical Institute. He also maintained an interest in the circulating library and the Warrington chapter of the Auxiliary Bible Society.

He died in 1844, apparently a victim of his own doctoring. It was a death surrounded by tragedy, for within two months two of his children died of gastric fever. The three grave slabs can be seen in the burial ground of the Friends' meeting-house in Buttermarket Street in Warrington.

Joseph's range of business affairs gave his executors considerable problems but the sorting out and tidying up of business affairs is a Quaker speciality. His brothers and his son George agreed to let the soapery carry on as usual until the annual stocktaking. The lease in the corn mill passed to a new lessee and they also wound up the partnership with Winstanley in the corn and flour trade. The interest in the cotton mill was written off as a complete loss. The remainder of Joseph's estate was in shares and the value of these was added to that of the soapery and the sums raised from the corn mill. The estate was affirmed at just under £20,000.

Two of the holdings inherited by his son George were to be significant, being nearly £2,000 worth of shares in the District Bank, and £650 worth in the St Helens and Runcorn Gap Railway Company. It is reasonable to assume that this stake in the railway company was of assistance in heading off a threat to break up the soapery through the construction of a railway across Bank's Quay. Instead of this, it was finally decided to use only a small portion of Crosfield land next to the river. For this the Crosfields were given plots of land adjacent to their own and a sum of money which assisted in the immediate construction of buildings on this new site.

The Crosfields found themselves in a situation where a railway they owned in part and had assisted in its expansion now provided them with excellent transport facilities at the soapery. Distribution of their soap was now possible throughout the country by simple loading direct from their warehouses into waggons. Coal and raw materials could be bought in the same way. The future of the Crosfields soapworks was assured, and they proceeded in 1856 to acquire more of the land to the north of them – about 2½ acres for the sum of £1,500, and fourteen years later they completed their purchase of the whole of Bank's Quay field. In the same year they acquired the lease of half an acre to the south-west, and three years later in 1872 a further half acre of river frontage adjacent to the soapery. This period of expansion had been accompanied by the construction of new plant and in 1863 the corn mill had been taken over for soapmaking.

This expansion was stimulated by the general social and economic growth of the period. Great Britain was ahead of the world in its industrial development and its manufacturing potential. This potential was realized through liberal trade policies and the establishment of overseas markets through colonization. The increase in the population together with rising living standards had led to a growth in national consumption from about 24,000 tons of soap to 87,000 tons in fifty years. The best was still to come, for in 1853 Gladstone abolished the duty on soap and in 1860 import duties on raw materials were abolished too. Consumption doubled again during the next twenty-five years with national production reaching 150,000 tons by 1895. It was to double once again before the end of the century.

The Crosfield expansion was part of this growth and required fairly heavy financing, which was provided by a new partner, William George Goodwin, who remained with them for some ten years. Just as important was skill in business. George Crosfield was the guiding-spirit that built on the enterprise and innovation of his father Joseph. He was clever and extremely able, determined to push ahead and having the industry and skill to do so. He had a deep personal knowledge of the business, both technically and administratively, and like many other Quaker businessman kept much of the clerical work and accounting in his own hands. He was also a director of the District Bank, which probably secured his line of credit and a prominent shareholder in the Warrington and Stockport Railway which was absorbed by the L.&N.W. Railway in 1859. A curious feature of his involvement with the railway was that he was also its auditor. His heavy investment in the L.&N.W. Railway led to such a personal involvement that in 1875 he moved to London, after thirty years in Warrington, leaving the business mainly in the hands of his youngest brother, John, who on George's death in 1881, assumed sole ownership until his sons joined him towards the end of the century.

Important though commercial acumen might be to the Quakers, a capacity for stable management and the establishment of fair prices and efficient distribution systems are not enough in themselves. At the root of a business such as the Crosfields lay the product itself. Were the goods in demand? Were they of saleable quality? There is no particular evidence that Quaker products were the highest quality available and it is unlikely that the Friends desired that honour. More important to them was the consistent production of reliable goods of a reasonable quality to sell at a reasonable price to ensure continuing demand. Their attention was continually devoted to developments in processing that would increase quality whilst holding or even reducing costs. The Crosfield family was no exception and the growth in plant was in part a function of the introduction of new processes and techniques. The application of steam for heating and power interested the Crosfields at Bank's Quay as much as it did the Lloyds at Burton. They introduced piped steam for heating the pans, for melting and purifying tallow and oils and for causticizing the soda. Steam was also used for mixing scent and colours with the soap to create the fancy soaps, now called 'toilet', for a growing market in the 1840s and 1850s. Steam was used for pumping raw materials or for transferring liquids from one process to the next and, of course, driving engines. The introduction of steam led to a reduction of manual operations; it also changed the face of the works, creating mazes of pipes.

The Crosfields were among the first to introduce sodium silicate both as a detergent and as a 'filler' in soap. Created by fusing carbonate of soda with sand and charcoal, it had the appearance of 'soluble glass' but was most effective in increasing the detergent properties of soap. Its use was stimulated during the Crimean War by the high cost of importing Russian tallow. One of the greatest applied scientists of the time, William Gossage, patented a process using silicate of soda and palm oil in 1855. By 1863 the Crosfields possessed an established silica works, which meant they had obtained a licence to use the patented process. In 1857 they paid James Blake and Francis Blackwell of Liverpool £1,000 for an exclusive licence to their patented process which employed hydrated soap to neutralize acids and alkalis in the soap, obviating the necessity of a costly process to achieve that end. The result was a method of producing cheaper soap.

The company continued to hold its interest in Gamble and Crosfields at St Helen's and, to benefit from developments there, in 1877 they had a process operating, for example, which placed materials in a large cylindrical iron furnace lined with fire-bricks and rotated by steam power to assist in the ridding of impurities.

The Crosfields not only bought licences for others' patents, they also acquired scientific brains of their own. In 1881 a link was established with Brunner, Mond and Co., when John Crosfield became chairman of that Company. They had successfully introduced the 'Solnay' process for the production of soda into Britain. The Crosfields assisted the establishment of Brunner Mond financially, their investment proving very lucrative. In 1890 Dr Karl Markel, a well trained and intelligent chemist, transferred to Crosfields from Brunner, Mond and Co.

At that time they were experiencing considerable competition from the Lever Brothers' soap operation which had started in Warrington in 1885 before removing to Port Sunlight. Markel persuaded them to develop their chemical interests, rather than trying to compete with the more substantial Lever. He recommended that Crosfields should specialize – confining themselves to spin offs from soap manufacture, such as caustic soda, silicate of soda, and their latest interest, glycerine, which was recoverable from spent lye used in one of their other processes. Markel was also to assist in another chemical development, that of edible fats. German applied science was ahead of the UK at that time and in addition to introducing German scientists to the business, they kept abreast of market developments on the Continent and made sure of continuing contact with soap and chemical concerns in Europe. As a result Crosfields were able to obtain the Sabatier–Normann hydrogenation process for fat hardening and an agreement with the German firm of Henkel for the production of 'Persil'. They acquired sole and exclusive licences to produce other hydrocarbons for conversion processes for other soaps.

Markel's contribution was wider than this for he was instrumental in the rebuilding of steam boilers, maximizing the efficiency of fuel in water evaporation, transforming the manufacture of glycerine to produce the purest quality product in the country and the highest quality silicate, and in the decision to manufacture caustic soda for domestic sale.

One other technical development at Crosfields is worth the mention – they were amongst the first to install electric light by a five horse power steam engine driving a dynamo. It provided electricity for two or three hundred lights. At the turn of the century, Crosfields had developed into a technically diverse venture, offering a range of products, employing up-to-date chemical processes, and using modern methods of production. The only things that remained old fashioned were the buildings.

The principal market was the burgeoning domestic market of Great Britain. By the 1870s Crosfields were producing quite a range of soaps at varying prices. The cheapest was a brown soap aptly titled 'Economic' wholesaling at 13s. 6d. per cwt. At 19s. came a pale soap also named with nineteenth-century subtlety – it was called 'Common'. They were perhaps best known for their mottled soaps which cost between 23s. and 46s.

The commercial side of the business was taken over by Arthur Crosfield, the son of John Crosfield, after an extensive training in this aspect of the business as well as the practical art of soap making. He developed a team of sixteen domestic travellers and a network of sixty agents and correspondents overseas. The primary domestic market for the soap was the North of England, since convention decreed that markets in soap should relate to site of production. Information about overseas markets is scarce, but the *Illustrated London News* reported in 1886 that 'Perfection' soap was sold throughout the world and that 'Erasmic' soaps were also exported to India. It was reported by the *Warrington Guardian*, in classically innocent example of nineteenth-century consciousness that 'some of the most brilliantly coloured samples are not prepared for the English market. They are intended for export, being designed to take the native fancy in the foreign bazaar.'

These strongly coloured soaps were for China, Java, India, the west coast of Africa, South America, the West Indies, and the Canary Islands. Sea transport was extremely cheap and it cost little more to send a bar of soap to Brazil than to the other end of England. Crosfields used either British export merchants or commission agents in the countries concerned, and with their sixty agents mainly throughout the Commonwealth they were leading exporters.

It appears that the firm's employees were more happily situated than workers generally. People wash, even in depressions, and soap selling was not unduly threatened by cyclic downturns and within that industry Crosfields, through their diversification into chemicals, were more soundly based to meet difficulties. Arthur Crosfield was proud of the fact that the concern had never lost a single working day, and he earned himself a reputation as a kind and considerate employer of labour. He knew most of his staff by name and provided pensions for long-serving employees. There was a sick fund in existence in 1868, and 200–250 workers went on a company outing to Llangollen in 1869 and over a thousand to Blackpool in 1883. In 1892, at a social gathering, Arthur Crosfield received an illuminated address as a token of respect and esteem which referred to his kindness and consideration, fairness, interest in the welfare of the workmen and his efforts to promote a harmonious atmosphere.

This was no mere sycophancy by the workers. It was the first such meeting in the history of Warrington. It should be remembered that at this time the Crosfields had, for several years, been speaking out in favour of trade unions, seeing organized labour as a necessary complement to capital though there was more than a degree of paternalism in the relationship of the Crosfields to both their workers and the town in which they lived.

This was inevitable, yet contained none of the Calvinistic notions of predestined superiority often associated with successful Protestant entrepreneurs. Their sense of position was based on having achieved as a family enough skill in production, enough expertise in business management, to have created an enterprise which had a significant status as an employer of local people in Warrington. It was a two-way process since both workforce and community at that time looked to the leading manufacturers and merchants for much of the necessary social philanthropy. It was a nineteenth-century ethic which is far less acceptable in the welfare state of today.

The Crosfields did not only contribute to the social well-being of those for whom they felt responsible because it was expected of them, or even because of enlightened self-interest. As Quakers they were a deeply religious family, active in the affairs of their society, and as such sharing the Friend's sense of Christian responsibility to their fellow man. The responsibility of one Friend towards another's suffering had widened with the cessation of that suffering. Yet this very standing in society was to draw individuals away from the Society towards the Anglican establishment. During the latter part of Joseph Crosfield's time with the Company, individual sons left the Society for the Anglican Church. As members of the established Church, we find them urging the unity of the Christian sects, the right to religious freedom and denouncing Anglican bigotry and injustices that had caused their predecessors so much anguish.

Joseph himself, in the exercise of his paternalism, supported many non-denominational activities, such as the Warrington Branch of the British and Foreign Bible Society and the Town 'Mission'. The Mission was an agency for education as well as religious instruction and Joseph contributed towards the cost of its development. In 1897–9 he leased land on which he built an infants' school. He was naturally opposed to Foster's Education Bill in 1870 because of its threatened Anglican domination of school boards, and ten years later opposed the establishment of such a school board in Warrington because of the sectarian animosity it would cause. He believed strongly in non-sectarian education and advocated the control of education by local councils, in whose hands education is today.

At the same time he was opposed to the municipalization of the local gas and water concerns. His sense of freedom which in the case of education led him towards municipal control, led him in the other directions as well. When it came to enterprise he believed that municipalization would be a burden on the rates and would operate less efficiently than private enterprise. Yet where he approved of public enterprise he supported it most positively, contributing generously to the Warrington Dispensary and Infirmary, to a large public hall and to public baths. Most significant was his contribution of enough money to enable the town to purchase Bank Hall and its grounds for conversion into a town hall, park and garden.

The Crosfields were active local councillors and magistrates, but more important than that was their role in party politics. Quakers have traditionally tended towards social democracy as a political response to the authoritarian attitudes of the aristocratic Establishment. Not only would this have sprung from their own mistreatment by the Establishment, but also from the fact that they were representatives of the new middle class. As merchants and manufacturers of the bourgeois Industrial Revolution they were responsible for much of the country's wealth and resented the traditional political influence of the landed gentry.

The Crosfields, like many Friends, were active in the Liberal cause. Since 1832 they had turned to the working classes for a coalition of capital and labour, a union of the useful and the industrious against the non-producing, rent-charging, royalty-exacting landowners. The Friends' antagonism was deepened by the fact that Tories represented the interests of the section of society they were morally opposed to, the brewers, the imperialists and the warmongers. Throughout the middle and later part of the century the Crosfields advocated further parliamentary reform, urging the extension of the franchise to the working classes, the re-distribution of seats and vote by ballot.

Their great victory came in 1868 when a Liberal was returned for the first time in Warrington, something for which the Crosfields had worked hard and contributed much. In 1869 the Liberal *Warrington Examiner* was published and the cause was firmly established in the town. The Crosfields continued to be active for the rest of the century and on various occasions themselves stood unsuccessfully as Liberal parliamentary candidates. Despite their own antagonism towards the ruling class, their social democratic instincts only took them so far along the road of individual freedom and self-determination and in two generations we find that the radicalism of Joseph Crosfield diluted into a 'We made good so why can't you' attitude on the part of his grandsons, particularly Arthur, who felt that socialism would be 'public plunder'. He believed that it would deprive of their property those men of enterprise, thrift and industry – the backbone of England. He denounced strikes and maintained that socialism was contrary to man's individualism and competitiveness. It was the classic liberal stance, fully conscious of the inequalities of society, yet believing that this could be resolved in time within the system as it stood. There was no contradiction in their own wealth – they had earned it and it formed the capital on which their workers depended.

The introduction of the laws of limited liability made outside investment feasible and weakened the bonds tying the Friends to their business. There was also a crisis of identity from the middle 1850s onwards that took many Friends out of the Society and into the Anglican establishment. This was not merely the response of individuals finding themselves with more wealth and power than it was compatible for a Quaker to have – many Friends like many other Protestants were able to maintain a simplicity in their personal lives divorced from the wealth of their business. It was simply that their success and local status brought greater and wider social pressures. As leading manufacturers and businessmen their positions brought them into contact with a wider range of social contacts that had to be maintained, despite the fact of these contacts being outside of the Society. Likewise, their philanthropic, social, and political activities brought them into continuing contact with the Establishment.

Joseph Crosfield's grandson Morland married 'out' of the Society to the daughter of a local solicitor who when he died in 1875 left £90,000 to his sons who devoted their lives to sporting pursuits. Morland's partner John Crosfield also married 'out' – to a family of Ulster Protestants. He retired to a large house and gardens at Walton Lea which he occasionally threw open to the public. He left £155,490 in shares in Crosfields and Brunner Mond Co. Ltd.

As with the Lloyds, the story of Joseph Crosfield and Sons, as a Friendly enterprise and Quaker family dynasty draws to an end with the advent of limited liability status. As the partners or proprietors grew old it was no longer necessary to dissolve partnerships and they were able to achieve a corporate permanence in their business. In addition they were able to gain legal benefits as well as investment for expansion. In the 1890s John Crosfield, the senior partner, was in his sixties. His three sons were all involved in the management side of the business but the stimulus to new products and processes provided by Markel demanded new investment capital. Their great competitors, Lever Brothers and Gossage and Sons, both incorporated themselves in 1894 and so in 1896 Joseph Crosfield and Sons Ltd was registered too.

It was really only after the Friends relinquished control over their businesses, and often their connection with the Society, that their enterprises grew into the major corporations we know today. They grew precisely because of the introduction of new styles of management and new investment. It is worth remembering that enterprises such as that of the Crosfields were, at the time of their incorporation, major ventures within their own areas of influence and equally well known at the time as the corporations that have developed out of them since. They represented the peak of nineteenth-century commercial development – the private enterprise venture capitalists ploughing back profits to create new capital for expansion – where expansion was financed out of income. These ventures could not have survived as industry leaders in the twentieth century with the development, first, of corporate enterprise backed by independent investment finance and secondly of public enterprise financed by the taxpayer. To have survived the nineteenth century, to have a company worth incorporating, depended entirely on the foundations laid by the earlier generations of Friends as leaders of industry.

There would have been no basis for development without the willingness of the originators to do without personal gain, to risk all, in creating their enterprise, or the solid talents of second-generation proprietors in providing service at reasonable prices, in running the business properly, in acquiring technical knowledge, the developing of good employee relations, the establishing of a solid relation with the community they served. The capacity of third-generation proprietors consisted in knowing when to diversify into new areas of activity and in some cases, when to leave the initial business behind.

Following the incorporation the shares were initially held by the Crosfield family, with Dr Karl Markel, whose scientific and technological ability made him indispensable. Incorporation allowed them to issue debenture stock for £150,000 at 4½ per cent. This was set against assets of over £300,000 and trust deeds held by two trustees. There was little difficulty experienced in raising this sum, which was used for meeting the cost of extensions so that the company could meet the demand for its product. The following year further capital was raised, this time to acquire three outside companies, the Titan Company, Keelings, and Medleys. Another major capitalization took place in 1898 with the establishment of the Erasmic Company to take over Crosfields' trade in milled toilet soaps, shaving sticks and perfumes. This wholly-owned subsidiary required a nominal capital of £100,000 to finance the attempt to break into the luxury toilet trade.

The central Company still retained Crosfields as chairman and vice-chairman, but to the other members of the family on the board were being added an increasing number of experts, many of whom had come up through the business itself. This reflected a growing hierachy of heads of departments and managers. By 1908 the Company had principal groups devoted to secretarial and commercial affairs and works and manufacturing. Between them they accounted for no less than thirty-three departments. The Company continued a policy of developing its own talent to the extent of disposing of most of the imported German expertise in 1907. Scientists were brought in at a fairly high level, but more important, Crosfields took the fairly radical step of taking this personnel from the research departments of British universities. These were added to the fast-growing number of technical, administrative and commercial managers being deliberately selected and 'trained up' from the Company's own personnel.

The enlightened self-interest of Crosfields' forebears in establishing adult educational facilities in the town paid off for the Company during this period. Training 'for the job' would only take selected individuals so far – the availability of evening classes to further technical understanding completed the task. For the right person there was not just the the chance of becoming a head of department but also the opportunity to reach the very top and Crosfield employees not only became directors of their own Company but of other enterprises in the industry.

The attention of Crosfields to employee relations in the form of employee incentives, general working conditions and social facilities was rewarded by the determination of their highly skilled workforce to remain abreast of technological development. They acquired pre-eminence among British soapmaking firms for their expertise in chemical research and technology. Lever Brothers may have cornered the market in promotion and marketing but Crosfields were technical masters. It was this expertise which allowed Crosfields to develop from the production of soaps where raw materials were rising at a prohibitive rate into, first, chemicals and second, vegetable oils.

To facilitate development in chemicals the Company developed a close relationship with Brunner Mond, which reduced their own need to invest large sums of money in producing the raw materials they required, and which Brunner Mond provided at preferential rates. In addition to caustic soda, the Company began in 1907 to produce Portland Cement, which within four years was producing a profit of £4,000 per annum. Silicate of soda required by the soapery was also marketed as a material on its own producing a profit of over £14,000 in 1910–11. Crosfields were also the largest UK producers of glycerine which returned a profit of over £80,000.

To facilitate this growth two further capitalizations had taken place in 1905 and 1911, giving a total share capital of £700,000. In 1912, Crosfields ceased to exist as an independent entity. The cut-throat war with Levers made it essential for them to protect their supplies of raw material, and in that year Crosfields ordinary shares, value £250,000 paid up, were exchanging for those of a similar paid-up value owned by Brunner Mond and Co. As the latter were quoted on the Stock Exchange at over four times their face value, it meant that Crosfield shareholders received nearly £1.1 million. The exchange found further capital for expansion, the strength to stand up to Lever Brothers, secured raw materials and a fat profit for members of the family. It also meant the end of the independent family business and the influence of the Crosfields over it.

The loss of their independent status led to a loss of identity. The First World War and the period following took the Company with Brunner Mond into extensive international competition, and all its complexities, with Levers, Jurgens Schidts, Proctor and Gamble, B.B.O., and others. These complexities led to conflicts of interest and the abuse of trading agreements. A high court action by Lever Brothers against Brunner Mond in 1917 resulted in an agreement to allow Levers to acquire half of Crosfields' shares (they were by this time associated with Gossages who had also been acquired by Brunner Mond) and the right to nominate a third of the directors of Crosfields and Gossages.

Levers had thus infiltrated the structure of Brunner Mond through 'Crossages' as Crosfields and Gossages were known, and as rivals were in a position to exploit the situation. It was also the case that the Company required still further expansion to survive. This would hardly happen whilst Levers were in a position to prevent it. It was in the best interest, now, of all concerned to allow Levers to purchase the rest of the shares in the Company and this happened on 8 October 1919.

The story of twentieth-century soap oils and chemicals is almost synonymous with the establishment of the vast Unilever Corporation. The merger of Lever Brothers–Jurgens, and Van Den Berghs, pushed Crosfields further down the hierarchy, and made them more vulnerable to rationalization. This process took a couple of decades, finally establishing Crosfields in the specialized role of chemical manufacturers. In 1960 their soap-selling interest went into a single organization, Lever Brothers and Associates Ltd, along with those of Lever Brothers Ltd, and Hudson and Knight Ltd. The manufacture of soaps was therefore concentrated at Port Sunlight. Soap flakes were to be produced at a new soapery at Warrington from 1962. From here are produced Persil, pre-eminent amongst its rivals, and Surf.

There were now two factories at Bank's Quay – one for Crosfields' chemicals and another for the soap powders of Lever Brothers and Associates Ltd. Crosfields have retained a leading role in the Unilever Group, largely as a result of maintaining that great tradition of technical expertise in chemicals, and economic production methods in soap production.

The old soapery buildings have been razed to the ground and the present chairman envisages a new soapery, technical centre and chemical plant, and where the soapery stood, a chemical warehouse has risen. Chemicals are big business in the modern world and one of the growth industries on which the success of Britain's economy depends.

CHAPTER 6

The Cadburys of Birmingham

The Cadbury name is a household word, totally associated with chocolate products, but also with progressive industrial relations, liberal democracy, and social welfare. Cadburys have been subjected to attacks by the government of the day for daring to threaten the existing monopoly over the press; they have been through the most difficult of times as a result of their Quaker pacifism and refusal to take arms in the First World War. They have not only survived, but retain today as bright and contemporary an image as at any time in their history.

Amongst the 750 products produced by Cadbury Schweppes Ltd are Cadbury Dairy Milk, Rose's chocolates, Hartley's Jam, Rose's Lime Juice, Dubonnet, Pepsi Cola, Jeyes Fluid, Ibcol, Smash and Marvel, and of course Schweppes tonic waters.

The Group has a total turnover in excess of £1,000 million. The Cadbury Trusts remain as active in social affairs as ever. Yet the story of the Cadburys is the history of a family and its relations with one town – Birmingham.

In Quaker families such as the Lloyds, or the Crosfields, it can be argued that their success was incremental – the result of layer upon layer of contribution from each generation, each relevant to its time and circumstances. In others, it is possible to identify a single generation or even an individual whose existence was critical to the ultimate success of the enterprise. George Palmer (of Huntley and Palmers) and Joseph Rowntree are examples. In the Cadbury story, Richard and George, austere Victorians, are the leading figures.

Richard Tapper Cadbury was born in Exeter in 1768 of West Country Quaker stock, but had served his apprenticeship with a draper in London. The family enterprise starts with Richard, for the Cadburys' enterprise belongs to the second consumer phase of the Industrial Revolution. It coincides with the period in which the Lloyds were in banking rather than their earlier involvement with raw materials and processing.

Richard went to Birmingham at the age of twenty-six to go into partnership in a drapery business. He married two years later and he and his wife moved into a comfortable house in Old Square, Birmingham. Like many Quakers, he was happy living over the business, for when it moved into an old inn at Bull Street the family moved into the same premises.

As a draper, Richard Cadbury was inevitably concerned with fashion and his shop became fashionable as a social centre where his clients would come not only to order garments, but also to meet, take wine and pass the time of day. There must have been an odd contrast between the business and its proprietor, as Richard dressed in the simple, severe style of the Quakers of the time. He was followed in this by his family and, apparently, as recently as 1905 his daughter was seen around Birmingham still attired in the formal Quaker way. The contrast would have been furthered by Richard's habit of holding regular bible readings with the staff and the fact that he and his family discountenanced all alcoholic beverages.

Over forty years he established himself, retiring in 1832 and moving to Edgbaston. He had ten children, who by this time were dispersed and in most cases married. His son Benjamin took over the business in Bull Street whilst another son, John, had for eight years been carrying on a tea and coffee business in the same street, having married Candia Barrow. Richard Tapper Cadbury was a personable and gregarious man, willing and able to give himself to both the Society of Friends in Birmingham and to his own family. Like so many provincial Quakers he was active as a positive influence in the social development of his town. He had educational interests, he was one of the Guardians of the poor, and a member of the Board of Commissioners, the then ruling municipal body of Birmingham, and was elected its chairman in 1836. All this happened at a time when Birmingham was growing at an unprecedented rate. This growth meant responsible and complicated work. Like many another Friend he accepted this responsibility fully.

Richard died in 1860, regarded as a kind man, an honest citizen, and a beloved parent. His son John, who was born in Bull Street on 12 August 1801, was fortunate in being the middle child of the family growing up in a stable environment and yet free of the pressures that would have been on his elder brothers. He was sent to serve a seven-year apprenticeship in the grocery business with a friend at Leeds named John Cudworth, and on completion of his apprenticeship, spent a year in the Bonded Tea Houses. A long and steady apprenticeship had to be served away from home, followed by a period in London to acquire experience of a wider world.

John was twenty-four when he took over the tea and coffee business, his father placing a sum of money at his disposal with which he would sink or swim. He was as shrewd as he was painstaking. The windows of his shop were bright and attractively arranged, usually by himself, and his industrious attention to business compelled the admiration of friends and neighbours. He never asked his father for further financial help.

In 1826 he married Priscilla Dymond from his father's town of Exeter. They were very happy together, but after only two years of married life Priscilla died. John, grief stricken, threw himself into a visit to Ireland in the service of the Society of Friends. A great feature of Quaker welfare work has been its commitment to the problems of the people of Ireland – in famine, poverty, and strife, even to this day. John with many other young Quakers went at the time of the potato famine that wreaked such misery in Ireland. This visit marked the start of his active association with the Society.

By 1830 he had become clerk to the local meeting of the Society and in the same year entered public life by being elected a member of the Board of Commissioners for Birmingham. He was to become chairman of the committee appointed to see the Bill through Parliament that transferred the power of the Commissioners to the new Corporation of Birmingham. Like his father, John Cadbury found himself involved in the public administration of his town, the affairs of the Society of Friends, and the great social issues of his day. He was appointed one of the overseers of the poor and was so enthusiastic in their cause that he upset many of his less progressive associates.

There were personal motivations for all this activity, particularly after his first wife died. He had been devoted to her and he took part in public life in compensation for the loneliness that he felt. Then in 1830 he met Candia Barrow whom he married in 1832.

It was a good marriage from John's point of view. Candia's father was a foreign merchant, having several ships which traded with the West Indies and John furthered his business interests. The tea and coffee shop had been operating by this time for a little over ten years. In 1835 he took a significant step using a warehouse in Crooked Lawn where he first experimented in mixtures of cocoa and chocolate with pestle and mortar. He moved this warehouse in 1847 to Bridge Street, taking into business his brother Benjamin and it was at this stage that the firm took the name of Cadbury Brothers.

There are strong similarities in the early history of the Cadburys of

Birmingham and the Rowntrees of York. Just as the Tukes were to separate their grocery interests from their cocoa warehouse, leaving it in the hands of Henry Isaac Rowntree, so John Cadbury took a decision to separate his tea and coffee shop interests from this new development in the preparation of and marketing of cocoa.

In 1849 the shop in Bull Street was handed over to Richard Cadbury Barrow, his nephew. John Cadbury did not totally abandon his interest in tea and coffee but gave up the day-to-day running of the shops to give increasing attention to the manufacture of cocoa and chocolate which was finally to absorb their entire trade. To the cocoa business came not only a brother Benjamin and a nephew Richard, but also his sons Richard, George and Henry. The new venture had six Cadburys as directors. In 1855, for the second time in his life, he suffered the shock of the death of a wife. It brought on a severe attack of rheumatic fever, from which he never entirely recovered. In 1861 he handed over the business to his sons, Richard and George, and spent the later years of his life in religious and philanthropic work. John Cadbury had in many ways satisfied the functions of the second generation of a family business. He had taken his father's resources to establish a new venture, and with patience and diligence had built up a business from the profits. With typical Quaker enthusiasm for new technology and new processes, he had experimented with techniques in developing a new product in chocolate and cocoa which finally came to dominate all his other interests. With the usual Quakerly concern for education and responsibility, he had trained a number of his children in the fundamentals of the business so that they could take over from him. He died in 1889, aged eighty-eight, and was buried at Whiton cemetery.

So we come to the third generation of the Cadbury family, that of Richard, born in 1835 and his brother George.

Quakers can no more choose their parents than anyone else. Perhaps George and Richard of the third generation would have preferred not to have owed anything to their family. Nonetheless they were born with many advantages. To a Quaker, however, it is more important to use these advantages properly and to accept the responsibility that they bring. They grew up in a happy and well-off domesticity. Their childhood coincided with the early years of the reign of Queen Victoria. No longer were men drawn by horses or conveyed by sailing vessels. Now they travelled in the steamship and the railway. The electric telegraph stretched across the land and under the ocean. The revolution in communications was no less sudden and no less complete in Victorian life than that produced by the advent of the transistor and computer in modern society. The grand junction railway from Birmingham to Manchester was opened when Richard and George were very young and almost at the same time the first train puffed its way from Birmingham to London. Their childhood was spent in a charming country cottage that their father had taken in Calthorpe Road. They had several brothers and sisters. Many of the accounts of their childhood written by Richard and his family indicate a life that was almost blissful. At the age of six Richard was sent to the Friends' boarding school at Birmingham, before joining his brother, John, at Charlbury School a few days before his eighth birthday. In November 1849, a year notable in England for a terrible epidemic of cholera, preparations were made for Richard's elder brother, John, to join his cousin, Richard Cadbury Barrow, in the family business in Bull Street. The decision to put John into the shop with his cousin Richard was accompanied with the usual careful consideration and deliberation by the family. Richard had a couple of years left at school at Hitchin. It had been similarly concluded that Richard would enter the family business at Bridge Street and the correspondence from his parents is full of advice as to how he should prepare himself for his adult life. On leaving school, he was sent on a tour to Switzerland by his father both for the pleasure and education that his visit would bring. The close of the Swiss tour marked the end of Richard's boyhood and his entry into the family enterprise. Richard settled to work at Bridge Street with apparent energy and devotion.

The products of the firm were beginning to gain recognition. The exhibition held to accompany the meeting in Birmingham of the British Association in 1849 contained Cadbury products. The item in the catalogue reads, 'Chocolate, Cocoa and Chicory, in various stages of manufacture, contributed by Cadbury Bros., Bridge Street, Broad Street, Birmingham'. The works at Bridge Street consisted on the ground floor of a storehouse, the roasting ovens, the 'kibbling mill' and other machinery. Above this was the packing room where a score or more of girls worked under the direction of a forewoman. They wore a kind of industrial uniform, their ordinary dresses being exchanged during work hours for a clean holland washing frock. This was an unusual innovation but gives an interesting insight into the concern of Quakers for the welfare of their workers. Everything was scrupulously clean and it seems that the workroom was a happy place. Endeavours were made to teach the girls habits of order and pleasant manners which might reach beyond their work hours to their homes and families. Once a week during the summer they were given a half holiday and twice a week they left an hour earlier than usual to attend evening classes. The male employees were encouraged to develop a steady habit of saving and virtually every employee from the mere force of the quiet example of their employers was teetotal. Such were the conditions of the Company in which John Cadbury's son, Richard, received his training.

There was an exciting event in November 1853 when the firm received the royal appointment as Cocoa and Chocolate Manufacturers to the Queen.

In April 1861 life introduced to Richard two major responsibilities. First was that of marriage to a friend of his sister. Her name was Elizabeth Addlington, a bright and graceful girl who was by all accounts accomplished, well informed, and a good conversationalist with attractive manners.

Her father, William Addlington of Mansfield, was a widely esteemed citizen and well-known member of the Society of Friends, and Elizabeth had received from her parents a thorough domestic training and was particularly skilful in needlecraft. Richard prepared a home for his bride in Weely Road and spent much of his spare time improving both the house and its garden.

That month also saw Richard and his brother, George who had joined him a short time before, installed as heads of the factory in Bridge Street. It was the start of a long business connection and friendship which lasted between the two brothers for nearly forty-five years. Their father's ill health had caused his frequent absence from the business and finally he was obliged to retire and leave it in the hands of his two sons. It was thirty years since he had first opened the shop in Bull Street now run by his nephew, Richard Barrow.

The new heads of the firm were quite young men, Richard being twenty-five and George twenty-two. The way ahead was full of difficulties, for the business was losing money, and for the next five years they were to have an uphill fight, with the double burden on Richard, who had not only to try to maintain the business but also provide for a wife and children. Both brothers had inherited money from their mother, and this they threw into the business. They decided, if it came to it, they would close down before there was any chance of a single creditor being out of pocket. Richard put down the value of everything he possessed not at the price he hoped to sell it but at the price it would fetch if it had to be sold under the auctioneer's hammer. This became the limit they were prepared to risk. Thus they prepared not only to fight but, if necessary, to lose. It was a sound principle that Richard followed throughout his business life and at no time were the debts of the business such that he could not meet them personally if called on to do so.

The first years of loss would have broken the courage of a less determined man. In his private accounts for the period, we can see his share of the loss on the trading of the Company, for the first three years. In 1861 his share was £226. In 1862 that sum grew to £304, whereas in 1863 his share of the loss on trading was down to only £20. These figures speak for themselves. Over that period the Company had lost over a thousand pounds, but efforts to reduce the loss were finally proving successful by the end of 1863.

There were many times when Richard had to face the prospect of abandoning the struggle and losing everything he possessed. His original private capital of £4,000 had been reduced to only £400. Plans were being made with George Cadbury to make a new start in life as a tea planter in the Himalayas, and Richard himself intended to take up land surveying. In the event these careful plans became unnecessary for in the following year, 1864, the business began to show a small profit and from this time it went forward with great strides.

This was due largely to their insistence, no matter how adverse the conditions, on running the business in the way in which they, as Quakers, felt was right and proper. Throughout the period of difficulty they were constructing a sound basis from which the business could then go forward into profit.

Richard always felt that, after his family, his first responsibility was towards those who worked for him and he regarded his workforce as being no less important to him than his capital. He never considered that his obligations towards them ceased when he had paid them their wages. The hours of work began at six a.m. A pint of coffee and a bun for the men and milk and buns for the women were always provided free of charge when they arrived in the early morning. If at any time they worked until after five in the afternoon, tea was also given. A great deal of personal attention was paid by the two young masters to determining whether individual employees had enough to eat and often they would send out one of the boys to buy extra food.

They visited their customers personally – a much more difficult undertaking in those days than under the present conditions of travel. Richard would often go into the warehouse and make up orders himself, not only in the early days but later on when the business was more successful. In addition to conducting morning Bible readings with their work people, they were generally a positive influence for good upon their employees by their personal commitment.

This spirit of Christian enterprise manifested itself until the 1870s in the relationships of Richard and George and their workforce. They were also active in Christian social welfare in the town of Birmingham, being concerned with education, poor relief and study of the Bible.

The success of the firm and the increase in the number of employees required larger premises and made possible the scheme which had long been near to the hearts of the Cadbury brothers. They dreamt of a factory out in the country where the work people could enjoy the benefits of fresh air and beautiful surroundings. It happened most fortunately that a small piece of land situated in a pleasant, healthy locality in Worcestershire near King's Norton was available, and the purchase led to the decision to abandon the works at Bridge Street. Building operations were begun at once and the world famous Bournville sprang into being.

The new factory at Bournville was easily reached by rail and canal from the great centres of commerce and its natural position rendered it a most desirable site. In the mid-nineteenth century it required a certain vision to appreciate the implications for the future, particularly of rail transport. The district was also healthy, the air pure and the water good and plentiful. The estate covered some fifteen acres and the firm decided, with typical practicality, to build the factory on the part nearest the station. Construction began in 1879 on three acres and plenty of room was thus left for extension when required. There was a pretty trout stream known as the Bourne which passed through the estate and the town by the stream became known as Bournville.

A cricket and football field was provided for the men, and a wide playground for the girls, fitted with swings and other contrivances for outdoor enjoyment. They built sixteen semi-detached houses close by the factory and bordering on the road at the southern side of the works. These were inhabited by the foremen and others and though both large and roomy with a front and back garden, the rent charged was only five shillings a week. Behind the houses was an orchard which they planted with apple, plum, pear and cherry trees. And the stream itself was widened into a pool in which an open-air swimming bath was constructed.

Inside the works large dining-rooms were provided separately for the men and women, and in the kitchen gas-stoves and cooking apparatus made it easy to provide hot dinners. The kitchens had a capacity to produce eighty chops simultaneously in ten minutes. Throughout the factory order and regularity prevailed, with special attention being paid to hygiene. This meant continuing with the policy of providing special washing dresses for the workgirls. Initially the material was provided free of charge for the first dress and the girls were required to start work in a clean frock every Monday morning.

The Cadbury brothers took enormous pleasure in the changes they were effecting and entered into every detail of the arrangements. 'We consider that our people spend the greatest part of their lives in their work, and we wish to make it less irksome by environing them with pleasant and wholesome sights, sound, and conditions.'

The employees themselves shared in the pleasure and greatly looked forward to the removal to the new premises. Richard Cadbury would conduct parties of the workgirls to their new destination, buying all their tickets and, as the train drew near to Bournville, eagerly pointing out landmarks to them. It was in a state of happy flutter and excitement that both employer and employees alighted at the station and walked up the lane to the new factory which was to become almost a lifelong home for so many of them. Neither, however, could have realized then the large development that was to take place at Bournville on the other twelve acres.

The partners had adjoining offices which looked out on a pleasant garden with rosebeds and shrubs. It was a great contrast to the outlook of their dingy offices in Bridge Street. They had realized that on coming to Bournville a large part of their lives would be spent in these rooms and they felt it would add beauty and strength to their work were these rooms and the outlook to be pleasant to the eye. Richard Cadbury took great pleasure in laying out the garden and supervised much of the activity that took place in landscaping. He seldom arrived for work later than eight thirty in the morning and would normally arise from his bed before seven in order to ensure that he could spend half an hour in the garden followed by family Bible reading at breakfast. He would insist on walking at least half of the way to Bournville where he would meet one of the works' letter vans which would give him a lift the rest of the way. Until the last few years he insisted on walking back the whole of the two miles at the end of the afternoon and rarely was his own carriage ever seen at the works. His attention to detail was particularly noticeable in the way in which he dealt with his correspondence. He never regarded this as a chore to be disposed of as efficiently as possible. He wrote a bold, readable hand and excelled in rapidity of composition and in accuracy. He knew what needed to be said and he expressed himself with clarity and precision. The volume of correspondence which he undertook meant that his kindness of heart and, frequently, more substantial tokens of his sympathy reached a wide range of people who had ventured to appeal to him on matters that were quite often outside the range of the daily business routine. He gained a reputation for extraordinary promptness in replying to every letter he received. It is as well to remember that he sustained exactly the same regime in dealing with personal letters to his own widespread family as he did in the business.

There are endless anecdotes about his approachability and his friendship with many of his employees. They show him to have been a charming man, and of equal charm are the photographs of his girl employees at the factory and in the grounds at dinner hour. Much of what Richard Cadbury set out to do from purely personal conviction and Christian charity was also very good business practice and whilst it would be cynical to refer again to enlightened self-interest, none the less the return in business terms of their investment in human relations was very considerable indeed. Every one of the innovations at

Bournville – buildings, equipment, processes, personal relationships and industrial relations – has served as a model for countless commercial enterprises throughout the world. Certainly Hampstead Garden Suburb and Welwyn Garden City were inspired by what John Cadbury did in Bournville.

Richard Cadbury's interest in Bournville affairs never slackened. Over the next thirty years as regular as the clock he would turn up every morning in the works' letter van. He published a book towards the end of his life called *Cocoa – all about it* (by Historicus). This is the first comprehensive work ever published on the subject; chapters on the history and the cultivation of the plant itself are followed by the history of its use as a food with subsequent chapters on its analysis, manufacture, its value as an article of diet and its adulterations. A description of vanilla and an appendix giving further particulars to the planting and culture of cocoa complete the book. Its publication aroused a great deal of interest and Richard had taken infinite pains that it should be as attractively presented to the public as possible and not merely a learned dissertation on a food product and its manufacture. For him to have done this is as complete a demonstration of Quakerism as it is possible to find. The intimate and loving attention to technical detail for the sake of intelligent understanding as much as for its relevance to the business runs through every page. The book received a massive press notice and the general verdict was that it was both entertaining and instructive.

During those last years at Bridge Street changes had taken place in the quality of the goods they manufactured. The 1872 Adulteration of Food Act created a precise definition of what could be added to pure cocoa. From this time the firm discontinued the production of the cheaper kinds of cocoa usually known as 'pearl cocoa'. This meant a severence of a very large part of the trade and it was felt to be worth the risk of loss in one direction in order to be able to speak of the cocoa they sold as being absolutely pure.

Bournville was becoming a small town in itself. Many trades were represented in the various departments, and the work of building and enlargement was continually going forward. The pleasant meadows by the trout streams were swallowed but the greenness of the country remained wherever possible to hide the bricks and mortar. The Cadburys were interested in landscape and concentrated on adding touches of bright colour in the form of creepers, flowerbeds and windowboxes. Intelligence and taste were manifest inside and outside the factory. By this time the extent of the works was considerable, with acres of warehouses and workshops divided by streets connected by bridges and intersected by railway lines. But for all this the first impression was that of entering a garden.

The Wedgwood factory, Etruria,
as seen in *Staffordshire and
Warwickshire Past and Present*,
J. A. Longford,
London, n.d.

Josiah Wedgwood,
1730–1795.
This portrait appeared in
Lives of the Engineers,
Samuel Smiles, Vol. I,
London, 1862.

Coalbrookdale, 1779. Darby's Iron Bridge as featured in *Lives of the Engineers*, Samuel Smiles, Vol. II, London, 1862.

A sketch of the Joseph Crosfield & Sons' soap works, Warrington, in the 1830s.

The soap factory in 1878.

A general view of the soap works of Joseph Crosfield & Sons Limited, taken from *The Illustrated London News*, 13 November, 1886, and showing: (1) the factory from outside with (A) the glycerine plant (B) the silicate plant, and (C) the alkali plant; (2) a soap display at the Liverpool Exhibition; (3) the frame room; (4) stamping out the cakes of soap; (5) the packing room; (6) the making of boxes, and (7) Crosfields' brand mark for Perfection soap.

The Cadburys of
Birmingham. Richard Cadbury.

George Cadbury

Women at work in the Cadburys factory, packing boxes of cocoa, c. 1890s.

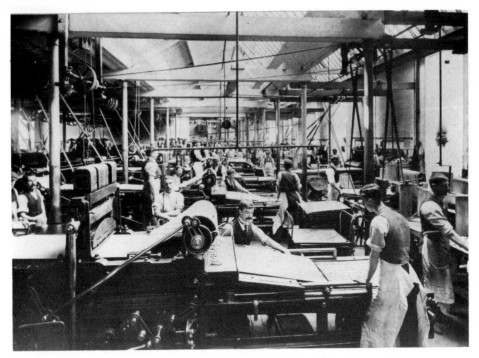

The Huntley and Palmers' biscuit factory, Reading. A view of the men cutting out biscuits in 1900.

The staff of Huntley and Palmers pose during a company picnic outing, c. 1900.

Henry Isaac Rowntree,
c. 1870.

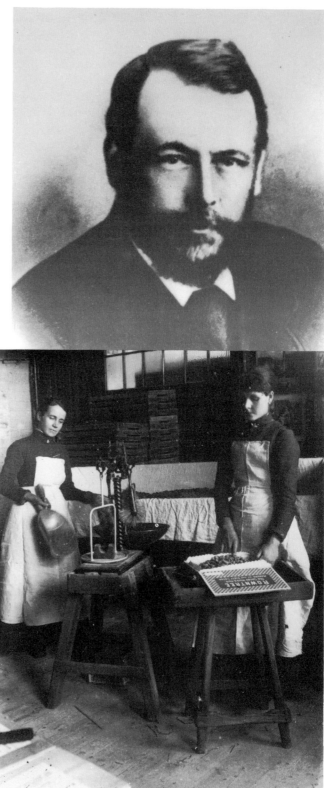

The laborious task of
sorting pastilles at the
Rowntrees factory,
Lendal Bridge, North
Street Works, York,
c. 1900.

Women packing King Edward VII Coronation tins at the Rowntree factory in 1902.

William Allen,
1770–1843.

Daniel Bell
Hanbury,
1794–1882.

By degrees the firm was able to purchase more of the land surrounding the factory. This included on the opposite side of the road an old family mansion standing in beautiful grounds, the name of which was changed from Bournebrook to Bournville Hall. It was not, however, to become the residence of the employers but more typically a home for about sixty of the workgirls who lived at a distance. Once again Richard was responsible for an innovation that would be endlessly copied – a workers' hostel. They boarded there altogether, or if they wished went to their own homes over Sundays. Richard took a personal interest in furnishing the Hall, particularly in the choice of pictures for the walls. Part of the gardens was railed off round the house and reserved for the girls, whilst the kitchen garden and vineries were used to provide comforts for employees who were ill and for whose care two sick-nurses were engaged. The rest of the grounds belonging to Bournville Hall were made into a recreation facility for the workgirls in general. They contained playing fields with tennis courts and a roomy pavilion. There was a belt of fine old trees through which attractive walks lined with rustic seats were constructed. The whole garden was reached from the main factory grounds by a tunnel constructed under the road and on a summer's day there can have been few prettier sights than the stream of white-robed girls who revelled in the sunshine of the open fields or sat in groups beneath the shady trees enjoying a picnic lunch.

Beyond the mere comfort and pleasure of the employees these surroundings contributed largely to the general air of health and cleanliness which pervaded the whole factory and which, of course, are of such importance in the preparation of food.

The system of payment adopted was known as 'piece work', employees being paid by the amount of work they did. From the first, the workforce was encouraged to save and on the occasion of the Queen's Diamond Jubilee, a savings' fund was established at Bournville. The sum of £1 was given to every employee who had been in the service of the firm for three years or more and ten shillings to those employed for a shorter time on condition that this should form the basis of an account opened for each one of them in the new savings' fund. At the end of the year the amount due to each deposit and interest of four per cent was transferred to the Post Office Savings Bank.

As the factory grew from employing hundreds to thousands it was not possible for George and Richard to be responsible for all the work and detail that went into creating the enterprise. It was the product of much co-operation and collective thought and its development was very much an organic evolution rather than a pre-planned growth. There were by the 1890s four members of the next generation of Cadburys at work. These were Barrow Cadbury, William Addlington

Cadbury, both sons of Richard, and Edward and George Cadbury, the sons of George. Each of these became responsible for some phase of the business and together with the original partners they developed the scheme of industrial welfare which made Bournville famous. Many of the details of this scheme are to be found in Edward Cadbury's book *Experiments in Industrial Organisation*. Bournville to George and Richard was never simply an isolated and self-sufficient experiment. George's eye in particular always scanned broader horizons, and Bournville was to him a model and a place where his ideas could be tested for wider use. The methods of George and Richard were rooted in sound economics, as opposed to mere philanthropy, their approach at Bournville being addressed as much to the business community as it was to any other. The problems of industry were tackled by the employers themselves. They did not wait for Parliament; on the contrary they gave the government inspiration, ideas and examples. Too often since the war in this country, business has blamed government for not taking steps to ensure their success and yet again there are isolated examples of enterprises where industrial relations, care and imagination, go far beyond a statutory requirement of the various industry Acts.

The achievement at Bournville was the result of infinite labour and self-denial. After the 1860s it was open to the Cadburys, as to other manufacturers, to incorporate their business as a limited liability company with shares issued to the public and quoted on the Stock Exchange. In other cases the transference from private to a form of public ownership weakened the obligation of Quaker families to the firm and modified the discretion of the directors. These enterprises ceased to possess the characteristics that in fact made them successful in the first place. The Cadburys refrained from such an incorporation at this time. Apart from the fact that the business would have belonged to others as well as themselves, they realized that they would become managers rather than proprietors. Incorporation might realize their fortune and relieve them of responsibility, but at the same time it would imperil their great experiment. Money for its own sake had no appeal for them and social ambitions were outside the scope of their thought. Their task, to make Bournville a solution to the social and industrial problems of the day, could not be delegated and this implied a policy of personal management. The vicarious conduct of industry through foremen who are the only persons to know exactly what goes on in their departments frequently produces not only grievances but even scandal and waste. The Cadburys were never satisfied with secondhand information and their policy, motivated by social considerations, reacted on the business efficiency of the enterprise.

It was during the 1890s that the burden of responsibility for the Company devolved mainly onto George Cadbury, and it was during this decade that Richard died. In 1895 George began another task, the full achievement of which is the Cadburys' most remarkable contribution to the history of their time. The germ of the scheme lay in their original decision to move from Birmingham to the open fields four miles away. There remained the problem of housing the employees, and most of them still lived in Birmingham.

The increasing status of the works with its many ancillary facilities and social schemes produced in the workers a desire to live closer to Bournville. By the 1890s the business had been considerably extended. The sheer force of economic necessity was bringing people into the area and it was inevitable that the works should become the centre of a large population. George Cadbury saw this, and knew that were it left to private interests to exploit, the very evils from which the workforce had fled in Birmingham would reappear. There would be fierce speculation in the neighbourhood and property values created by the presence of the factory would be exploited by speculators and jerry builders. Public houses would spring up at every street corner and at the end of all Bournville would be the centre of a new slum area. The decision of 1878 to move to the country would have been in vain.

George Cadbury's desire to provide an object lesson in housing was reinforced by the immediate need of saving industrial experiment from disaster. George Cadbury conceived the concept of the garden city, which has become a commonplace today. The garden suburbs, towns, villages and cities, Hampstead and Letchworth, Wolverhampton and Rossyth were mainly due to the demonstration which George Cadbury gave at Bournville that slum conditions are not a necessity of our industrial system.

He started from a sound practical principle. He believed that if the principle was right so would be the result, and with a sure instinct for the essential began in 1895 by purchasing 120 acres of land in the neighbourhood of the works. This area gradually increased to over 800 acres. This step was to solve the whole problem of housing and town planning and he employed the most competent professional advice, consulting anyone whose experience was valuable. It was George himself who supervised the experiment and controlled the main lines of its development. He planned the roads, the groupings of trees, elevations of houses, widths of pavements, the amount of garden space, the proportion of land devoted to park and playgrounds. It became the work of years, work exactly suited to his genius for combining social advantage with practical necessity. He did not deny that the work had a value for his business. Indeed, it was part of his scheme to appeal to the self-interest of the businessman as well as to the mind and thought of the community.

The Cadburys were fortunate in being their own capitalists. The surplus finance required for their industrial and social experiments was created at Bournville. George Cadbury was able to find all the money which his scheme required, and he was thus able to concentrate on the detail of planning and architecture. He began by building 143 houses which he sold at cost price on a lease of 999 years for the ground on which they stood. His idea was that the tenure should be made as nearly freehold as possible but the conditions of the lease made it impossible that the gardens should be destroyed or built over. Half the purchase cost was advanced at the rate of $2\frac{1}{2}$ per cent interest and loans in excess of this half paid interest at the rate of 3 per cent. No single individual was to hold more than one acre or six houses. A condition of the loans was gradual payment by the purchasers. Thus in the case of a cottage costing £150, the householder would pay £30 in advance plus twelve yearly payments of £10 plus £23 of interest paid over twelve years. The total sum thus paid was £173. This set against a normal rent at the time actually represented a saving over the period of some £10, whilst the tenant also secured a house, and with the house a garden of considerable value.

To begin with the leaseholders were able to obtain commercial advantage through reselling their houses, in one case at a profit of 30 per cent. This private enjoyment of unearned incomes was contrary to George Cadbury's intentions. At an early stage, therefore, the policy of the estate was changed in a fundamental respect. The whole area of 500 acres, including the village, was handed over to trustees under the control of the Charity Commissioners. The trust property at the date of gift was valued at £172,724, consisting of 370 houses. This grew over the next twenty-five years to 720 houses. George Cadbury's gift was absolute. He surrendered all private interest in the capital and revenues of the estate. The present trust acts as a constantly developing snowball and there are well over 1,000 houses on the estate.

The estate is not a charity. The tenants pay a fair, economic rent sufficient to defray interest on capital invested. The conditions attached to the scheme were few and simple. Each house must have a suitable garden, and no building may occupy more than one quarter of the land allotted to it. The roads must be ample and bordered by trees and at least one-tenth of the land in addition to roads and gardens must be reserved for parks and recreation grounds. The roads are 42 feet in width, the houses set back at least 20 feet from the pavement. The houses are not placed in long straight rows but irregularly with an eye to picturesque unity, each house occupying an allotted place in the general vista. Even factories may be built on the estate but the latter are to be restricted in area to one-fifteenth of the whole. No public house or building for the manufacture or sale or co-operative distribution of intoxicating liquor can be erected in Bournville without the unanimous consent of the trustees signified in writing. In the event of a public house being started the whole of the profits must be devoted to securing recreation and counter-attractions to the liquor trade as ordinarily conducted.

These are but a few details of the operation of Bournville village. It is impossible to estimate the effects of the experiment upon the moral and intellectual life of the community but its effects on health and physique are calculable. In its early years the differences between Bournville and the national averages in death rates, infant mortality, general health and weight of children were phenomenal. There must be very few people who doubt that George Cadbury's experiment at Bournville was anything other than an enormous social and cultural success. Like the factory they built twenty years before it quickly began to profit by its own dynamism, thus creating a reason within itself for its own existence.

In 1899 Richard Cadbury died on a journey to the East. To the end of his life he was busy with a new scheme connected with Bournville. This was the erection of thirty-three almshouses near the new model village. They were intended to prove of value to the aged employees of the firm who always had first chance amongst other applicants. The Cadburys would never put self-interest before need and over the years only a small proportion of the inmates of these almshouses have had any connection with the works. Richard also built a large adult educational institute on the Moseley Road at this time but he put as much interest into the new almshouses as though he had nothing else on his hands. The houses are typical of the Cadbury style. They are semi-detached, one-storey cottages round a quadrangle. There are gay flowerbeds and a clocktower which stands in the centre. The age limit was fixed at sixty years and over, and married couples could continue to live together. The dwelling was given free along with fire, heat, light, medical attendance and medicines. To build a permanent endowment fund for the almshouses Richard Cadbury built thirty-eight houses for ordinary residents, along the adjoining road, which were let at rents varying from £19 to £30 a year. Not for the Cadbury's the misplaced enthusiasm for establishing a venture that could not sustain itself in the years to come.

It is inevitable, given the successes of the Cadburys with their factory and their model village, that the story of the Cadbury family in this century is one of dedication to a reign of social and moral causes. Like so many other Quakers their names are mentioned in every aspect of public service and in liberal politics. Cadburys were involved in temperance, in justice, in education, particularly adult schools and mission work, and many other philanthropic ventures both here and overseas.

The Boer War diverted the current of George Cadbury's life into new channels. Hitherto his activities had been confined to Birmingham and to his various business, social and moral causes. He was not generally known outside Birmingham except to Quakers and others engaged in philanthropic and religious work, who had found him a generous supporter and a pioneer of social ideas. He maintained what is now described as a low profile and tended to avoid publicity. This was partially due to modesty but also one suspects to his own conviction of the correctness of his approach and his sense of independence of all outside influence. His aim was to get things done, and he held the view that things got done only if the right instruments were chosen and if the perpetrators were indifferent as to who received the credit. He was often criticized for the secretive manner of his activities, but to him it seemed that power was only a means to an end and that his very abhorrence of publicity was an indication that he never sought power to increase his own status.

He had always been strongly impressed with the power of the newspaper to mould opinion and to exercise influence for good or evil upon the life of people. Whilst he understood a newspaper, like any other business, had to be conducted on businesslike lines, he felt that its responsibilities differed from those of ordinary enterprises and that its chief task should not be to make money but to bring an enlightened and public-spirited criticism to bear on events. He had, therefore, with this object in mind, purchased a group of weekly newspapers having a large circulation in the suburbs of Birmingham in 1891. The enterprise was a modest one and was entirely successful. The newspapers reflected George Cadbury's ideal and exercised a valuable influence on the life of outer Birmingham but at that time he was not tempted to go further. His life was Birmingham and he had no particular wish to carve out for himself kingdoms in spheres unfamiliar to him.

The Boer War was a convulsion in the life of the nation. The country was swept by a nationalistic, jingoistic frenzy, marching to the strains of the imperialist words of Rudyard Kipling. The eyes of statesmen had turned from problems at home to ambitions abroad.

The colonial and imperialist designs of those who had worked skilfully for the conquest of the Transvaal in Southern Africa were powerfully aided by the attitude of the press whose voice was overwhelmingly in favour of the war. The newspapers fanned the ignorant passions of the mob whilst giving no information at all as to the financial realities of the Boer escapade. Two morning newspapers had the courage to oppose the policy of the Government and the frenzy of the public. These were the *Morning Leader* and the *Daily Chronicle*. It was easy and profitable for the newspapers to create and then ride on a tidal wave of passion. The situation was grave from the point of view of those who opposed the war. In the middle of it, one of the two newspapers that had until then opposed the Government, the *Daily Chronicle*, changed its attitude, causing the resignation of the editor and several members of his staff. For the opponents of the war the situation was now intolerable, particularly since the Government and its supporters would allow very little opportunity for the expression of opposing points of view.

Lloyd George, one of the leaders of this opposition, saw that the struggle was hopeless without some effective backing in the press. His eye ranged over the possibilities and saw that the one hope was the *Daily News*. This particular newspaper had a history bound up with the cause of peace even though, in this particular instance, it was supporting the Government. The paper preserved an honourable respect for facts, in marked contrast to the general spirit of the press. It had, until the beginning of the war, been generally associated with the Liberal Party and at this particular time, having lost a great deal of political support, the paper was finding itself in financial difficulties and the proprietors were interested in disposing of their property. Lloyd George set himself to capture this powerful vehicle of public opinion in the interests of those who were opposed to the war, and he gained a considerable measure of support for his proposal.

He approached George Cadbury who was known to be strongly against the policy of the Government. George's opposition went further than the normal Quaker pacifist opposition to all wars. He took the view that it was a mine-owners' war, waged for financial interests, and that the public passion was being exploited in the cause of higher dividends and cheap labour. It was no light thing at this time to oppose the war in any part of the country, and particularly in Birmingham. Joseph Chamberlain's dominion over the Midland city was still unchallenged and he exercised for a generation an unparalleled sway over the great industrial community. During the war that influence was never more powerful. The Quakers are traditionally used to finding themselves because of their moral convictions beyond the social pale, but given the strong personal support that the Cadburys had in their own part of Birmingham, it is unlikely that George was unduly concerned. He threw himself with unaccustomed enthusiasm into local political struggles, resolving to undo Chamberlain's influence in their part of Birmingham.

So strongly did Cadbury feel the need that the public should be informed of the real facts of the origin and conduct of the war, that he should have warmed to Lloyd George's idea. He hesitated to take the much more serious plunge, which the acceptance of Lloyd George's proposal involved. The men of Birmingham are essentially provincial. It was in Birmingham that many of the initial developments began challenging London in the commercial and industrial field. Through the Lloyds it had seen the establishment of the first successful provincial banks, and to this day the commercial men of Birmingham retain a fierce provincial independence, preferring to finance their enterprises from resources, suspicious of decisions emanating from London, and ever anxious to continue the development of Birmingham as the commercial and industrial centre of the United Kingdom.

George would have been full of these provincial sentiments. In addition the recent death of his brother Richard had placed upon him, at a time of great personal grief, the additional responsibilities of the family and the business. His local interests in the adult school and other moral enterprises were very dear to him, and he would have seen a venture involving a London newspaper as being a totally new departure. Nevertheless, when he found that the scheme was in danger of falling through, he advanced the £20,000 required and the paper was secure. It was controlled on the business side by a board of directors, and on the editorial side by Mr Rudolph Lehmann. They employed many of the staff who had recently resigned from the *Daily Chronicle*.

The change in policy of the *Daily News* under its new owners created a powerful effect on the country. It became an impulse to the cause of peace, exposed the machinations of the mine-owners, and denounced the evils of the concentration camps and the executions that were taking place in Southern Africa. It also acted as a filip to Liberalism generally which revived under its energetic and audacious leadership.

This awakened a bitter reaction in the Government party, and the paper suffered disastrously from a loss of advertising revenue. Firms which had had dealings with it for years shut their doors against its representatives and this was one illustration only of the general boycott. Divisions also began to appear in the board of directors, so hurriedly brought together, and at a time of severe financial loss these divisions became accentuated.

Matters came to a head when Mr Thomasson of Bolton who, like George Cadbury, put up £20,000 for the enterprise found that he was in such fundamental disagreement with his fellow directors that he could not continue his connection with the enterprise. George Cadbury was left with a choice of personally unacceptable decisions. He neither wished to assume new responsibility in regard to the paper, nor did he wish to see it pass into other hands and revert to its original attitude on the war. He shrank, at his time of life, from so heavy a burden, but the decision was taken that he should take over the newspaper. He was convinced that it was his duty, and he was certain in his own mind that to make it successful he should leave the management in a single competent control.

He negotiated successfully with a north country journalist who had considerable newspaper successes in Middlesbrough and Blackburn, and had recently been associated with the establishment of the *Daily Argos*, an evening newspaper run in the Liberal interest. This was Thomas Ritzena, a man in strong sympathy with Cadbury's own social ideals, above all a keen land and housing reformer. Between them Cadbury and Ritzena took two decisions that had an important influence on the course of events.

The paper should contain no betting advertisements or forecasts, nor any racing news at all, nor should it accept advertisements for liquor. There were some differences of opinion between Ritzena and Cadbury on this last point. Millions of good people, said Ritzena, consume intoxicating drink, but he knew of no earnest Christian worker who gave way to betting. The paper began its new career with these two serious restrictions.

It was a well-intentioned but mistaken experiment. Had the restriction been confined to the mere exclusion of forecasts, no harm would have been done but the exclusion of all racing information represented a far greater restriction and whilst it was welcomed in some quarters, it was resented in others as an unwarrantable censorship of public morals. It brought into question the whole question of the neutrality of newspapers on moral issues.

George Cadbury took little or no part in the conduct of the paper. He had satisfied himself that the only prospect of success lay in an unrestricted personal control, and he himself had neither the temperament nor the intimacy with the details of the newspaper business to exercise that control himself. His object to secure the advocacy of the *Daily News* for the social policies in which he believed had been achieved. From that point he left all the business details to the managing director and the control of policy to the editor.

George Cadbury, as proprietor, had taken on some considerable problems in relation to his newspaper. It had begun by losing a lot of advertising revenue as a result of its opposition to the popular policies of the Government. Its restrictions on racing information and advertisements for intoxicants had placed further limits on both its circulation and its advertising revenue. At this time, the introduction of the cheap halfpenny popular newspaper represented a further erosion of both circulation and advertising revenue in the more expensive one penny daily. George faced his problems with characteristic courage. He spared no money in his attempts to revive the fortunes of the paper, now at a very low ebb. Each edition was enlarged to sixteen pages, new machinery was installed, the building was remodelled and the whole administration overhauled.

The circulation was raised from 30,000 to 80,000 and its influence grew accordingly. At an editorial level it became synonymous with the new spirit of social reform abroad in the political community. Society was undergoing a great change, and there was now immediate concern about the social conditions of the people. The *News* sponsored an exhibition of sweated industry, held at Queen's Hall, which remained open for six weeks. The workers, who were restricted to those employed at home on piece work, sat there plying their trades at a pace which left no illusion that slackness could have been the cause of the smallness of their weekly wage.

The effect was deep and lasting. The national conscience was awakened and the ordinary consumer began to realize that tolerance of the system under which such wages were possible was a crime. Employers of labour were startled in many cases to learn what the system of contracting and sub-contracting really meant and out of the exhibition emerged a Bill for a minimum wage in a sweated industry. This Bill became law under the title the Trade Boards Act and applied the principle of the minimum wage to three or four specified sweated industries. The success of the Act led later to the extension of the system to a great number of industries in which the workers were too ill-organized for ordinary trade union action.

No less important was the campaign which the *Daily News* conducted for compulsory powers for the establishment of smallholding which bore fruit in the Act of 1907. The paper associated itself very powerfully with all kinds of social and industrial interests. It was not only a vehicle for mobilizing opinion, but also for initiating action. George Cadbury also underwrote the cost of a religious census of London. The results of the census created a deep impression and surprised the Churches with valuable knowledge.

The *Daily News* also played a conspicuous part in the Bethesda strike. This was the culmination of a long period of strain in the relations between Lord Penrhyn and his workpeople. Penrhyn was despotic in his conception of the rights of ownership and was prepared to suffer any loss rather than yield to his workers, who, as a result, were equally stiff and uncompromising. For more than a year the strike represented a tragedy without parallel in British industry. The Bethesda resources were dependent entirely on the great quarry and with these resources withdrawn it had no means of existence except those that could be raised from outside. The *Daily News* opened a fund and formed a committee in London. Through this fund and the effort of the Bethesda choir which toured the country something like £30,000 was raised. The *Daily News* campaigned for arbitration, but the struggle only ended with the complete exhaustion of the men and the destruction of their union.

The winter of 1904–5 was a time of grave unemployment and distress in the East End of London. Work in dockland was negligible and Canning Town was reduced to a state of impoverishment unexampled even in a district where extreme poverty was a normal condition. The whole region of the docks and West Ham fell into the grip of famine and a few days before Christmas when it was clear that unless food was forthcoming the people would perish, the *Daily News* opened a fund for their relief. A series of powerful articles gave a poignant picture of the famine-stricken homes of West Ham. The public response was instant and munificent. Throughout the Christmas season cheques and postal orders rained into Bouverie Street. Local committees were formed in every ward in south West Ham. Relief was given in kind and clothing and warehouses were established to which the gifts of goods were sent and from whence they were distributed. The immediate pressure of famine was relieved and the *Daily News* assisted in the search for work for the unemployed. As a result the unemployed dockers were given useful public works at the expense of the *Daily News* fund. Old playgrounds were asphalted, and new ones laid out; an open-air bath was constructed; West Ham Hospital was painted and decorated; levelling and draining work was carried out in Epping Forest and in many directions useful and permanent work was accomplished.

In all these enterprises Cadbury took a deep interest and to all of them he gave generously. But the general financial position of the newspaper was becoming increasingly unsatisfactory; the enlargement of the paper had added substantially to the cost of production whilst the advertising revenue showed no signs of increasing. Losses grew steadily more formidable and it became doubtful whether the paper had any kind of future. It was then decided to change the format of the *Daily News* to that of the halfpenny newspaper and the change was made promptly and successfully, in spite of great mechanical difficulties. The result was an increase in the circulation of the paper and wider extension of its influence. The self-imposed handicaps in relation to gambling, racing and advertisements for alcoholic beverages became even more acute in the new format, which was geared to a much wider circulation, and the demands on George Cadbury's purse rapidly increased. He had already sunk a great portion of his capital in the paper although he had never intended to profit by the money that he had invested. None the less, he could not contemplate a permanent loss of up to £30,000 a year, especially as he knew that he would have to provide for his family on his demise. He could have sold the property, but it would have meant the transfer of its political influence to causes with which he did not sympathize and he took the view throughout that his money was better spent in influencing public opinion in the direction of social reform than in any other cause. He decided to carry on, but it became clear to him that he must make a change in the control of the business. In 1907 the manager, Mr Ritzena, retired and was succeeded by George Cadbury's third son, Henry Tyler Cadbury, who gave up a farming career at the request of his father, and with his friend, Bertram Crosfield, who had married Eleanor Cadbury, undertook the task of management under a board of directors of which his eldest brother, Edward Cadbury, later became chairman. They took a bold decision to make a new advance on popular lines. The decision was for simultaneous publication in London and Manchester. Premises were taken in Bale Street, Manchester. Machinery was installed there and a duplicate staff established. The two officers were connected by private telegraph wires and the paper was issued simultaneously from the two centres. In this way the paper was brought within reach of the entire country from Cornwall to Aberdeen in time for the breakfast table. The result was a further very large increase in the circulation which was now approaching 400,000 per day. But the cost of production was proportionately increased and the losses continued.

The struggle for new financial viability of the *Daily News* had now become the dominating interest in George Cadbury's life. He had entered into it unwillingly and it had brought him nothing but financial loss and abuse. He became the target for the attacks of all who hated the new social policy pursued by the Liberal Government after its return to power in 1906. That policy had been created, advocated and made possible largely by the influence of the *Daily News*, and its opponents struck at George Cadbury as a most effective way of attacking his paper.

The more he was slandered the more he became convinced that it was his duty to continue the struggle. He had no personal aims to further and was satisfied that the policy of the Government was right, and in supporting it, he was doing the best service to his country that lay in his power. He never looked for rewards and was philosophical about the attacks upon himself. In 1910 he advanced still further into journalism. At this time, the *Morning Leader* and the *Star* were both on offer by their proprietors. They were both Liberal newspapers and George Cadbury was anxious that in changing hands they should not change their policy. It was known that Conservative concerns were interested, and in order to defeat that possibility, George Cadbury

agreed with members of the Rowntree family to buy up the proprietors. They knew that they would be attacked for acquiring these
papers yet they went ahead.

The *Morning Leader* and the *Star*, in common with other London
papers, published betting and racing news. To exclude such news
from them would have ruined them and they would have been
open to attack that they had deliberately destroyed such papers in the
interest of the *Daily News*. Cadbury was fully conscious of this
dilemma and decided that the *Star* with betting news and pleading for
social reform and for peace was far better than the *Star* with betting
news and opposing social reform and stirring up strife with neigh-
bouring nations. He consented to take some part in the purchase but
with the idea that in the course of years it might be possible to do
without betting forecasts. There followed a furious campaign against
George Cadbury and the Rowntrees in a certain section of the
Conservative press, headed by the *Spectator*.

Week after week there were attacks on him through which the
charge of organized cant and hypocrisy ran like a refrain. He was
reviled as a sleek hypocrite who profited from opposing evil. The
truth was that he had spent a large fortune on newspapers and to the
end of his days never drew a penny of personal profit from them, nor
had he ever any intentions of doing so. The lead of the *Spectator* was
followed by other newspapers and for some months there was an
outcry. The *Manchester Guardian* commented, 'The Cadburys and
Rowntrees are assailed with such severity and in tones of such severe
morality that a careless reader of the controversy might have supposed that they had introduced a gambling newspaper for the first
time into the white-robed company of the London daily press instead
of having made almost the first break with that disreputable practice.'

George Cadbury was also becoming the subject of criticism within
the Society of Friends for having taken over a newspaper that was
associated with racing and with betting. He had to take the middle
way – that way which often pleases nobody – and hope that in due
course reform could be accomplished. Now well over seventy, he
was physically alert but no longer fitted to bear the mental stress
which problems of conduct always gave him. Every act was the
subject of grave thought and as he advanced in years it made a heavy
demand on his nervous energy. He began to be troubled by attacks
which formally would have left him indifferent and when the question arose of amalgamating the *Daily News* and the *Morning Leader*,
he decided to surrender his interests to younger hands. He had steadily maintained that no personal profit should accrue to him from his
newspaper interests and had devised his property in the papers in
such a way as to secure that the principle of the application of profits

to public causes should continue after his death.

He forwarded a memorandum to his sons who would be concerned with the future of the paper as trustees of a new trust he had specially created in order to protect the principles on which he wished the paper to proceed in the future. In 1901 only 39,000 copies of the *Daily News* were issued each day. In ten years of strenuous work the circulation had been massively increased. There were years of loss, struggle and disappointment, yet at the end of it he looked back with intense joy and satisfaction to the expenditure of time, energy and money on the newspaper. The memorandum was his formal farewell to the enterprise. With the amalgamation of the two morning newspapers and the circumstances that apparently assured success, he saw no personal role for himself from that time on.

George and Richard Cadbury were primarily responsible for establishing the name Cadbury not only as a household word but as one synonymous with social justice. George's wife Elizabeth was to become Dame Elizabeth Cadbury. Throughout her life she was actively engaged in various women's movements and in the furtherance of her late husband's social and philanthropic schemes.

By the early nineteen hundreds both George's sons, Edward and George, and Richard's sons. Barrow and William Addlington Cadbury, were in the Company. The latter was also to become Lord Mayor of Birmingham from 1919 to 1921. The business by then employed nearly three thousand people, compared to the two hundred and thirty employees at the turn of the century. The Company was given limited liability status as a private company in 1899 and in 1912 Cadbury Brothers became a public company. An amalgamation of the interests of the Cadburys with those of the Frys was carried out in 1919 through the inauguration of the British Cocoa and Chocolate Company. The total workforce today at Cadburys exceeds 40,000 and the Board of Directors still contains members of the Cadbury family.

CHAPTER 7

Huntley and Palmers of Reading

The name of Huntley and Palmer is as synonymous with biscuits as the name Cadbury with chocolate and cocoa. Once again the origins can be traced to the watershed of modern English history, the aftermath of the Civil War. In Gloucestershire, close to the Oxfordshire borders on the eastern slopes of the Cotswold hills, lived a line of yeomen of the village of Oddington by the name Huntley. John Huntley is recorded to have been reported to the ecclesiastical authorities in 1682 for not attending church or receiving the Sacrament. It was a time of major agricultural depression and he and his wife Sarah were descirbed as being very poor. They took a decision in common with many of their time to leave the land and seek their futures in the towns and villages.

Whether their nonconformity expressed itself formally in membership of the Society of Friends is not certain. Their grandson Joseph certainly was an active Quaker. The son of John and Sarah had become a barley merchant and had done sufficiently well to give his son Joseph a reasonable education. He was to move to Burford in Oxfordshire to take up schoolmastering – one of the professions that did not require the taking of an oath and was therefore open to the Quakers. Like many another, Joseph headed for a town which avoided petty persecutions of Friends. Free of such restrictions, he was able not only to pursue a career as a schoolmaster but to develop his philosophical interests, he became first of all an elder of the local meeting of Quakers. He published philosophical tracts and in 1742 was elected to the highest office of the Society, clerk of the London yearly meeting. He was the first of four generations to become elders of their local meeting – the fourth generation being represented by Thomas Huntley, who was to go into partnership with Samuel Palmer.

The educational tradition of the family was endorsed in the next generation when Joseph's son, Thomas, became headmaster of one of the most important Quaker schools in southern England, Hillside Academy at Burford. He was a competent scholar, but more important, he insisted that his pupils were taught double-entry book-keeping and given a general commercial education as well as some elementary science at a time when the public and grammar schools were concentrating on the classics. Thomas married twice. His second wife, Hannah, was a woman of much spirit. She bore him eight children and brought up two step-children. In addition she was active in the ministry of Friends as well as acting as matron of the school. Her energy and practical business sense provides us with another clue to the antecedents of Thomas Huntley, for she found time amidst her other activities not only to rear pigs but to bake biscuits in the school's large oven. The bacon went to feed her many charges and very occasionally to be seized by the parish constable for non-payment of church rates. The biscuits had a more interesting destination. The school, Hillside Academy, is so named because it lies at the top of a steep hill above Burford. It was necessary for coaches to stop on the way down to put on the drag, and on the way up for horses to regain their wind. Hannah would go out of the school and sell her biscuits to the travellers in the coaches. Little could she have realized where this small piece of commercial enterprise would lead in the future.

Thomas's father was a man of big ideas that often required a considerable amount of money, but he was fortunate enough to make a good marriage. His wife was the granddaughter of a wealthy Quaker malt-ster at a time when Reading was one of the most important malting centres in England. Mary Willis had inherited her grandfather's freehold shop, a large granary and a malthouse by the River Kenet and some property held on long lease in Reading.

It was partly due to her interests in Reading and partly due to the failure of his various activities at Burford that Joseph and his wife moved in 1811 with their four young children to Reading. Despite the failure of his various activities previously, and contrary to all traditions of the Society of Friends, Joseph obtained an established position in Reading's Quaker community. On the basis of a certificate despatched at the time of his move and which testified that he was free of debt, he was at once accepted at Reading as a minister. Within two or three years it was discovered that Joseph was unable to afford the expense of educating his children. Moreover he had been in this situation since the time of his move. Given the enormous emphasis placed throughout the history of the Society of Friends on propriety in all matters relating to business dealings, the discovery of Joseph's insolvency must have shaken the rather staid local Reading Quakers. Fortunately just at the time when matters between Reading and Banbury were appearing to come to a head Joseph bounced back into solvency by an inheritance and his problems were solved.

Soon he was in trouble again. Joseph and Mary had been living off the interest from her grandfather's trust. In the year 1814 a combination of economic misfortunes struck Reading. It began badly when communications between London and Reading both by road and by water were halted for twelve weeks. There had been a particularly poor corn harvest and the abnormally dry autumn so lowered the levels of the canals and rivers that boats could not get to and from London. Reading's trade was so depressed the creditors there were forced to call in their debts. Joseph's solvency evaporated in the wake of his pressing creditors and the family was reduced once more to poverty.

Had Joseph's credit-worthiness not been destroyed then his son, Thomas, might well have become the fourth generation to enter school-teaching. He was a gentle and scholarly man who clearly took after his grandfather, the headmaster of Hillside. As soon as he was fourteen years of age, however, instead of staying at school and training for a profession as a schoolmaster he was taken away and sent like many other young Quakers to be apprenticed in Epping to a Mr Benjamin Doubleday, a grocer. After spending two years with him, Thomas moved to Uxbridge where he lived with his uncle, John Huntley. John had a bakery and a biscuit shop just off Uxbridge's High Street and he remained there until 1822 when, fully trained, he returned to Reading. His father decided to take advantage of this training and Joseph and young Thomas opened a biscuit, bakery and confectionery shop. Joseph managed the business and kept the books while Thomas did the baking and his sisters served at the counter and made themselves generally useful. In November they took a shop at the southern end of London Street, a few minutes' walk from their home.

Thus the business from which Huntley and Palmers developed was founded in November 1822 under the ownership of Joseph Huntley. The customary technical skills of the Quaker enterprise were vested in the abilities of young Thomas. Upper 72 London Street still exists, although it is now twice as wide as it was in 1822. Then it was only 18 feet wide but the premises went back a long way with a large underground bakehouse and a covered alleyway at the side. It was one of three biscuit-baking shops in Reading and one of thirty other bakers in the town. An idea of the modesty of their business may be gained from the fact that initially a sack of biscuit flour lasted for six months and each day they used less than a quart of milk for their biscuit making.

The Huntley shop was opposite the Crown Hotel, a posting inn on the thoroughfare between London and Bath. There were three coaches each day to the West Country and another three returning to London. Like his grandmother before him, Thomas found his biscuits being sold to what today is still described as the 'carriage trade'. Prices in the inn were atrocious and the fare limited. Travellers resting at the Crown would often cross to the little shop across the way in order to buy refreshments for the journey. There is evidence that they were to stock not only biscuits but Jacob Schweppes' mineral waters. Thomas's father resourcefully conceived the idea of sending the delivery boy with his basket to sell biscuits to passengers waiting round the inn yard while the horses were being changed. The travellers, having tasted the Huntley biscuits at Reading, began to demand them from their grocers at home. The market for their biscuits was suddenly enlarged, and the Huntley business began to grow.

Joseph enlisted the help of Thomas's younger brother, Joseph. The boy had been apprenticed to a Reading ironmonger and then sent away to complete his training in the Black Country, the centre of the iron trade. On his return in 1832 he had opened a shop next door to the Crown Inn and opposite the biscuit shop. His father now persuaded him to make tins and tin-lined boxes which solved the problem of keeping the biscuits fresh. This was particularly relevant to the carriage trade where until now those purchasing biscuits had only been able to keep them fresh for two or three hours. Joseph also took a leaf from the book of the owner of his own shop, one James Cox. James Cox had invented a sauce that was popular enough to be sold throughout the United Kingdom. Joseph learnt a great deal from his neighbour about the methods of distributing household products and in the 1830s there is a record of James Worth, the first Huntley traveller, dealing in several commodities including the Huntley biscuits. It comes as something of a relief from the often monotonous puritanism of other Quaker entrepreneurs that Joseph combined his travels in the ministry of Friends with the exercise of selling his biscuits on the way.

By the late 1830s the firm was doing well and selling some twenty different brands of biscuits, ranging from the Captains and Oliver varieties to more choice cracknels, macaroons, and sponge tea-cakes. It made four kinds of cake, apart from the rich bride cakes which were made to order. The other three were all produced in batches according to demand. They had one or two other items of confectionery and it may be seen from the first surviving account book for the year 1837 that turnover for credit accounts came to £1,410, to which there might be added another £200 odd for cash sales over the counter. The practice of keeping the books in his own hand was certainly carried out by Joseph and there were some 117 customers, seventy of whom can be identified as grocers being situated in fifty-two different towns or villages scattered over a wide area of southern England. All these localities could be reached by the various canals and water routes or were in carrier distance from Reading. The Kent and Avon Canal transported the Huntley biscuits to Bath and Bristol and along the Bristol Channel to Bridgwater, Newport and Ross on Wye. The Thames carried biscuits to the Medway towns of Rochester and Aylesford and the Grand Junction Canal took them to Hemel Hempstead, Aylesbury and Buckingham. Navigation led to other markets but in the main the economies of canal travel ensured that the goods travelled by water instead of by road.

In 1838 Joseph Huntley, afflicted by paralysis, retired, and Thomas, although an excellent tradesman, did not really possess the ability to manage the business side entirely on his own. It was necessary for him to find a partner to take his father's place and also to provide extra capital for expansion in the future. But it was to be three years before Thomas was joined by Joseph Palmer, an enterprising and energetic young partner.

The Palmers were entirely a West Country family. They had made a living as tenant farmers at Long Sutton in mid Somerset. There had been a branch of the Quakers in the district since well before 1670 when their old thatched meeting-house had been wrecked in a local persecution. By 1720 the Palmers were known to be Quakers. George's family had prospered on the land and his father and his uncles owned between them several thousand pounds' worth of holdings around Long Sutton. His mother had been born Mary Isaac, of a family of West Country tanners. Her mother, George's grandmother, had been a Clark from Street in Somerset – a member of the family that became famous for founding Clark's shoes. Mary Isaac had come to Long Sutton with all the inherited shrewdness of both the Clarks and Isaacs to run a shop in the village and it had not been long before her fair hair and brown eyes had attracted an offer of marriage from William Palmer. George was only eight when his father died. His mother decided that her sons should not try and make a living as tan farmers like their forebears but should be apprenticed to trades. His father's will had set up a trust to see to the children's upbringing, education and eventual apprenticeship. George Palmer was sent to a Quaker boarding school at Sidcott near Weston-super-Mare. He found the practical nature of his Quaker education quite stimulating. This consisted of grammar and geography, experimental lessons in chemistry and electricity and they awoke in him an interest in science and gave him a practical skill in engineering and mechanics. He left

Sidcott in 1832 and was apprenticed to an uncle in Taunton to learn the trade of confectioner and miller. He was encouraged to continue his education as a member of the Mechanics Institution at Taunton, and to develop the other major interest of his life, politics and public affairs. The most far-reaching event of his apprenticeship occurred during a visit he paid one day to Bristol. While browsing in the shop of James Busvine, a grocer, he bought some of Huntley's Reading biscuits and took them back to his master. Within four years he was to move with his mother and sister to Reading to begin the association with the Huntleys.

The story, probably apocryphal, has it that the decision to move to Reading was a result of a chance meeting between George Palmer and Thomas Huntley. The story tells how Palmer was on his way to London when he alighted at the Crown Inn at Reading, saw the biscuit shop across the road and entered into conversation with Huntley. Learning of Huntley's desire for a partnership, he straight away volunteered himself and so the association was begun. As others have pointed out, this story is unlikely, and yet the history of commercial enterprise is dotted with successes arising from opportunities taken at chance meetings, so perhaps it can stand as a pleasant legend.

Thomas Huntley and George Palmer concluded their partnership agreement on the 24 June 1841. It was to run initially for a period of fourteen years. The gross value of the business was estimated at just over £1,000, of which three-quarters represented debts owed by customers. Thomas Huntley's financial interest was computed as standing at £550 and so to this George Palmer now added an equivalent sum in three instalments. Thomas Huntley was formally recognized as the senior partner, and was to keep the accounts and ledgers as well as supervising the packing department. George Palmer was to manage the manufacturing department, where he would spend at least five hours a day. The remainder of his time was to be devoted to the general duties of the business, including sales and correspondence. He was to live over the shop at a rent of £20 per year while the Huntleys rented a house in a nearby street. His sister, Mary, became a shop assistant.

Despite this George Palmer took effective control of the business from the outset. He opened a bank account and deposited the takings once a week. At this time only eight people were engaged in the business, apart from the shop assistant and the travellers. There were the two partners, two craftsmen, two apprentices and two boys who assisted with packing and made local deliveries. There was virtually no machinery. George resolved to enlarge the premises by renting the shop next door and to increase productivity by introducing power-driven machinery.

George Palmer installed a powered machine on the ground floor. It was of no more than 1½ horse power and was intended to save labour in the dough mixing. It was successful enough to encourage him to plan the machinery for the factory which he aimed to set up in due course. His own apreticeship had been in biscuit-making but he had the special practical aptitude and interest in mechanical matters that went back to his schooldays and which encouraged him to seek new technology. He was fortunate to discover precisely the kind of technical adviser he needed in Reading. A rapidly growing enterprise in Reading was the iron foundry of Barrett, Exall and Andrewes. William Exall was a skilled inventor with a fertile imagination who relished developing and perfecting technical processes. George Palmer asked for his collaboration in mastering the technical problems of mechanizing biscuit manufacture.

George was more than just a technical man. He had a strong eye for the marketing and distribution side of the business as well. In addition to a growing series of public advertisements in newspapers rising to *The Times*, he also put his mind to the way in which the biscuits were being distributed. It will be recalled that the Company had employed Thomas Worth as a traveller, who had built up a network of retailers throughout the south of England and that Thomas's father, Joseph, had in his Quaker peregrinations, assisted in this matter. George Palmer decided to engage seven or eight commission agents in different parts of the country. They were not salaried, but combined the commission of seven and a half per cent from Huntley and Palmer with the commission they earned by working for other firms.

The result was a slow but progressive increase in turnover. In 1841 this was a little over £2,700. A year later it had risen to £3,360 and by 1843 it had jumped to £4,650. Increased turnover does not necessarily imply increased profits. With the establishment of a wholesale operation the firm had made a substantial investment and profits in the third year amounted to only £323. Over the three years money had been borrowed in small loans which amounted to £716. The firm was rapidly coming to the end of available credit and debts due by 1884 amounted to over one-third of the year's turnover. Like the Cadburys, Huntley and Palmer found that their struggles over the first three years produced a sudden minor but distinct encouragement. Their profits in the next year trebled to £969 representing 17 per cent of turnover. By then the number of employees had risen to sixteen and the increase in profits would seem to have been entirely due to the mechanization that George Palmer inaugurated.

It should be noted that mechanization without product is irrelevant and much of the profit that they made in 1844–5 was as a result of their perceptiveness in paying £50 for the right to make 'the patent unfermeted bread' produced by Henry Dobson of Southwark. They obtained the right to make and sell the bread within 5½ miles of Reading. In place of yeast the bread contained hydrochloric acid and carbonate of soda which generated carbonic acid for lightening the dough. Till then the only type of bread which the firm had produced were fancy rolls and the new bread proved an immediate success, making a substantial contribution to a gratifying rise in profits. In 1845–6 they exceeded £1,000 for the first time whilst the turnover was up to nearly £7,000. The partnership had come through the first period of its existence, but the risk-taking was not at an end, for George Palmer had resolved to set up a new factory.

The area to the north-east of Reading, hitherto undeveloped, had attracted industry as a result of linking the road from Reading to the intersection of the London and Wokingham roads. A number of factories had been built, including a brewery, a gas works, a tobacco factory and Messrs Baylis's silk crêpe factory. It had been opened in 1841 but it never paid its way. In mid-1846 George Palmer and Thomas Huntley negotiated its purchase for £1,800, which was lent to them by John Wheelan, a prominent Reading solicitor and property owner. The mortgage was to be repaid at 5 per cent. The site was level and there was a good wharf to take care of the riverborne traffic both for bringing the ingredients and other supplies and to carry away the finished product. The London road was also close by, and the Great Western Railway was but a few hundred yards away, connecting Reading not only with London and Bristol but also with Taunton, Oxford and Leicestershire.

The firm now had its opportunity to achieve substantial growth. The opening in 1846 of the King's Road factory was the crucial step in establishing Huntley and Palmer as a national enterprise. It was also critical for the establishment of biscuit making as an acceptable area of manufacture of which the country could be proud.

Very little organized biscuit making existed in the nineteenth century. Much of the major manufacturing of biscuits was done for stores and ships at sea and the 'ship's biscuit' remains a symbol of coarse and basic feeding to this day. The bakers, naturally, were situated close to dock-yards. Beyond these producers there were any number of ordinary bakers of bread who produced biscuits for their better-off clientele. The entire enterprise of biscuit making in the United Kingdom was fragmented, loosely organized and in its methods extremely primitive.

James Dodgson Carr was a Quaker who founded a milling and biscuit making business at Carlisle in 1831. He designed a machine for cutting and stamping biscuits, borrowing the basic idea from the hand-operated fly press developed by William Caxton the printer two centuries before. Carr's process, although in no sense automatic, led however to his being granted a royal warrant of appointment to Queen Victoria and, of course, today Carr's of Carlisle are still a great biscuit manufacturer.

Thomas Grant had in addition invented a form of machinery for ship's biscuits in 1829 that had proved so effective that Grant was awarded £2,000 by Parliament as well as a gold medal by the Society of Arts. Of the three, it was George Palmer who really put his mind to the problem of mechanical processing and details of his developments are admirably set out in T. A. B. Cawley's excellent book *Quaker Enterprise in Biscuits*. His developments included dealing with the problems of hard and soft doughs for different kinds of biscuits, a mixer for weighing and combining ingredients, and machinery for integrating the entire process. George Palmer was the most successful innovator of the Quaker biscuit makers, because his vision was broader. He not only understood the problems of production but also of business management and distribution.

When Messrs. Huntley and Palmer moved into the new factory at King's Road they did not immediately introduce a whole range of mechanical processes. It was a long-drawn-out period of settling in and an even more gradual process of mechanization. Output grew gradually from a weekly average of £120 on moving in to £175 in six months. In the same time the labour force grew from around twenty to nearly fifty workers. The partners had taken an enormous risk. In addition to the loans they had raised to finance the capital investment there was the general maintenance and upkeep of the new premises, far higher overheads and wages and technical problems as well. New premises and untried machinery would offer any business a set of unforeseen problems. It was essential for the business to raise its supply and its income as quickly as possible. In the first six months the weekly income rose to only £175. Six months later, by June 1847, they were turning out £200 of goods a week and later that year the firm was able regularly to achieve £250 per week. Their first full trading year showed a total output of £8,260. This represented a 20 per cent increase on the business they had done prior to moving into their new factory. Yet this in no way justified the move in terms of the capital expenditure and loan repayments involved.

George Palmer possessed that classic instinct of all entrepreneurs who chose to expand their way out of their financial problems by 'living' on their own increased turnover. During the 1847–8 period he met all his commitments, including the outstanding £600 for initial items, out of current earnings. In the following year he began paying off the principal of the original investment. This was to have a marked effect on the Company's profitability and in the second year of business turnover had risen to £18,000 – more than double that of the previous year. In August he reduced the prices of many of his products, thus boosting further the demand, although as a Quaker he may well have felt that his prime motive was to pass on savings to the customer.

Demand began to soar so rapidly that Palmer realized that he would never be able to satisfy his customers without a complete technical overhaul of the baking process. Despite the fact that his main process was mechanized, work at each end of the production line was done by passing materials to and from ovens by hand. He therefore devised a travelling oven in which products could pass through at a speed regulated according to the baking period required. It was to take him two or three years before, in 1851, he heard of a revolving oven for baking ships' biscuits made by a Liverpool company. The oven was 20ft long and 4ft wide and contained a feeding web on which boys placed the biscuits. In this way his baking processes were geared to meet the pace of the other portions of the manufacturing process.

The two stages of the industrial revolution – the development of basic material and transport on the one hand, and allied manufacturing and assembly on the other – had, as it were, created its own clientele. The new burgeoning middle class associated with the development of commercial enterprise was also a great consumer of the products of that enterprise. George Palmer was an expert in every aspect of his business and would not neglect the process of distribution or his customer relations. He had established in 1841 commission agents who by this time had in turn established a comprehensive network of retailers. In January 1847 there were over 700 retailers operating in nearly 400 different towns throughout the United Kingdom. George Palmer did everything he could to publicize the retailers of his biscuits and in every tin of biscuits a booklet was placed giving the names of the retailers under their respective towns. The vast majority of them were grocers and tea dealers, with a handful of bakers and confectioners. Several small post offices, and even some circulating libraries in watering places, also sold Reading biscuits. At the other end of the scale we can find the majestic Fortnum and Mason of Piccadilly who in 1846 purchased £127 worth of Huntley and Palmer's biscuits.

Palmer was typically enlightened in his relations with distributors by insisting on a number of requirements. First, they were to satisfy him with their credit-worthiness. Second, there could be no competition between distributors in any one locality. The firm also insisted that distributors should sell at recommended prices. The firm took action against a Southampton grocer who sold at a half-penny more per pound than the manufacturers recommended. As good business practice, Palmer saw that his retailers were getting an average of 20 per cent mark-up on his products. Certain favoured customers such as Fortnum and Mason received an additional discount of 5–7½ per cent. Finally, trade debts had to be paid within ninety days which was roughly the period between travellers' calls.

In the years after 1846 George Palmer spent most of his time on day-to-day problems as well as trying to look to the future. In addition to the travelling oven he oversaw the introduction of pan-type mixing machines and new types of cutters for the biscuits. A new counting house and warehouse were added to the original structure. The machinery and fixtures item in the accounts grew in ten years from less than £2,000 to over £9,000. With the gradual development of routine operations in the factory he was able to develop other aspects of his life. In January 1850, at the age of thirty-two he married Elizabeth Meteyard, the daughter of a Quaker druggist who was Huntley and Palmers' agent in Basingstoke. She was twenty-four. During the next fifteen years, she bore him ten children, four sons surviving infancy, three of them, in due course, entering the firm. Normal hours were worked at the factory on the day of the wedding and throughout the short honeymoon George was kept posted about the latest batches of correspondence and events in the works.

In common with Crossfield, Cadbury, Fry and others, George Palmer was to devise ways of showing his appreciation for the work done by his employees. One of these was the factory supper, usually held in April. Long tables were set out in the main factory building and tastefully decorated with plants and flowers. All employees, their wives or sweethearts were invited as well as numerous guests. After the supper some form of entertainment such as a magic lantern display would round off the evening.

By early 1850 Huntley and Palmers was established at a site where there was room for expansion, Palmer was attending to the necessary technical developments that would justify the use of such large premises, a distribution network of commission agents throughout the country had been set up and was working smoothly, and the workforce at the factory was established and settled.

Until then the company had been run by the two partners, Thomas Huntley and George Palmer. Relations between them were, however, deteriorating. George Palmer could claim justifiably that he not only had to carry out his side of the business but had also to compensate for his partner's neglect of the accounts. The ledgers were in a sorry state, columns were not totalled and errors remained uncorrected. Nor apparently was an accurate account kept of loans and their repayments by the business, thus giving a distorted picture of the actual financial situation of the Company. Thomas Huntley could claim justifiably that George Palmer, as an aggressive business man, was arrogant in his lack of consultation with his partner regarding growth and technical developments. Matters were further complicated by a disagreement between the partners regarding the entry into the business of relatives who would become partners.

George Palmer wished to bring his brother Samuel into the business as a manager with the prospect of partnership after four or five years. Thomas would not agree to this proposal unless his son, Henry Evans-Huntley, aged seventeen, was also given a similar opportunity to be taken into partnership at a future date. There was an obvious question regarding the relative merits of Samuel Palmer and Henry Huntley. The two partners could not agree and it was decided that the matter should be referred to three Quakers as arbitrators. This was normal practice within the Society of Friends and is a good example of the Quaker connection in operation. The business activities of the Friends were closely scrutinized by the Society, particularly when Friends got into business difficulties. Friends were expected, therefore, to accept the general ruling of a religious fraternity that had always taken a much closer interest than usual into the secular affairs of its members. The arbitration took a wider view than merely the question of relatives joining the Company. It also looked closely at the question of Thomas Huntley's role as the book-keeper of the business.

As a result of the arbitration some necessary reforms took place. A full-time book-keeper was appointed to relieve Thomas Huntley. His son, Henry, was to receive a professional training, while Samuel Palmer was offered a salary equal to one and a half per cent of the turnover entirely free of risk. He was to take charge of sales from the Reading office.

Although the arbitration sought to operate to the benefit of these young relatives, it ignored, in fact, their particular interests. Samuel preferred to live in London and be paid by results. He was not interested in one and a half per cent of the turnover and he was not interested in living in Reading. As a result he remained in London where he handled with enormous success the London and export trade for the company and also the purchasing of ingredients. It is clear that Samuel was very much a chip off his brother's block and it is quite likely that had he been at Reading, friction may well have developed between the two very positive personalities. As it was, he remained in London, led a busy life in the City, and enjoyed a stylish, if somewhat un-Quakerly existence.

This led to reorganization of the management at Reading and William Palmer was brought in to the firm to become factory manager. William was yet another brother of George Palmer and was a sterling character who was prepared to be reliable and dependable and to accept the rule of his brother George.

The transition to a new set of proprietors for Huntley and Palmers was established quite quickly during the year 1850. It was necessary, for George was in yet another expansionist mood. In the next two or three years he purchased a number of small pieces of land in the vicinity of the Reading works, including the tobacco factory next door.

During this period the firm continued to grow so that by 1857 the turnover of the company exceeded £110,000 per annum and was returning a net profit of 11 per cent. The budget of February 1857 set them on an even fairer course with welcome reductions in the import duties on tea, coffee and sugar, at the same time as reducing the income tax for their consumers.

It was in that year, however, that Thomas Huntley died. He was a man who had suffered considerable pain throughout the latter years of his life and therefore had not been the dynamic partner that he might have been. The history of Quaker enterprise is not simply composed of dynamic successful achievers. It could be argued that part of the story of the Friends in enterprise is concerned with the phenomenon of people being in the right place at the right time. Had Thomas Huntley not encountered George Palmer outside the biscuit shop or wherever they *did* meet, then the world-famous partnership would not have been forged. No doubt George Palmer would have achieved success in any case, but it is less likely that Thomas Huntley's name would have lived after him.

Thomas died leaving an estate of £35,000 and was mourned at his funeral by a workforce that now numbered 400. The partnership was automatically dissolved by Huntley's death in March 1857, and arrangements had already been put in hand for the management of the enterprise to pass into the hands of the three Palmer brothers, George and William at Reading, with Samuel operating in London.

There was the question of young Henry Evans-Huntley whom Thomas had been so anxious to bring into the business. The arbitration had required him to take a course of training and he had done a trial period within the firm. This did not prove a success and if the partnership had had any apprehensions that Henry might now claim a partnership their fears were soon set at rest. He declared that neither his health nor his inclination drew him towards conditions of 'punctual application to the business'. All he desired was to share the capital in cash so that he could buy some properties. The old partnership was wound up on 31 March 1857 and its value calculated. Henry received a proportion of the total net assets and retired to Dorset. He readily covenanted not to allow his name to be associated with any other biscuit firms. Under a new agreement of 19 October 1857, the business was given its present name of Huntley and Palmers. Samuel and William were brought into full partnership with George and each would henceforth be entitled to a quarter of the profits. Samuel removed the London office, eventually ending up at Rood Lane off Fenchurch Street.

The period from then until 1874 is characterized by the continuous growth of the Company. From 1857 through to 1874 the average growth rate of turnover was never less than 13 per cent. In one year it reached nearly 19 per cent. Thus it was that in 1874 the turnover of the Company had multiplied by six times to what it had been at the start of this new partnership. This can be measured in a number of different ways. The output of biscuits grew from 2,000 to over 12,000 tons during that period, capital reserves from £50,000 to £320,000, while the buildings and machinery grew in value from £27,000 to £113,000. The total profit during the whole period of the second partnership came to nearly £750,000, an astonishing amount of money during the middle of the nineteenth century. So far from needing connections to raise loans during this period of time, the partners even went so far as to lend money to their cousins, Cyrus and James Clark, when their shoe manufacturing firm fell into financial difficulties in 1863.

The growth rate was phenomenal, and credit should be given to the management of the three brothers. Together they represented a fair balance of the range of skills required by the business. George provided both technical insight and entrepreneurial drive, William proved to be a sound and reliable day-to-day manager on the manufacturing side, and Samuel displayed clear-headedness in the development of marketing, the purchasing of supplies, and the operation of company finances generally.

It is interesting to note that the Quaker connection did not always extend to an automatic association with other companies having similar interests. During this period the firm was busy converting its sales force from commission agents to salaried employees. They politely turned down an offer from Cadbury Bros. when they offered in 1851 to act as the Company's agents in the Birmingham area. George Palmer's own words are interesting. He said, 'We find that business done by ourselves is so much more satisfying than that done by commissions. If we make any alteration in Birmingham we are at present inclined to take the ground into our own hands.' It should not be supposed that the move to salaried employees was yet another way of cutting the costs of distribution because salaries were cheaper than the commissions that were then being paid. Huntley and Palmers of Reading were very good payers. In 1874 William Bullivant Williams earned £1,100 a year plus bonuses and holidays as the firm's bookkeeper and manager of the partners' personal financial affairs. Salaries paid to salesmen ranged from £160 to £350 a year for ordinary salesmen up to as much as £750 paid to chief representatives in 1874. These payments were substantial amounts, given average earnings nationally at that time.

The market was expanding. Though 23 per cent of the output was going overseas, it was not simply a working-class consumer market. The creation of an industrial economy had also created the demand for a wide range of services in commerce and industry. This demand was satisfied through the creation of a substantial group of people who today tend to be described as middle-class. Thus it was that during the middle of the nineteenth century domestic-consmer patterns were being established many of which survive today. Many English families were now eating different kinds of food and at different times of the day. More specifically this middle group of people were the major influence in effecting these changes. The poor, as always, were not in a position to alter their diet very much. The average earnings of working-class families in 1874 were probably around 17 shillings a week. Their disposable income for such things as cakes and biscuits therefore probably amounted to less than 2d. Substantial rises in disposable income were associated wholly with the middle class where the increase in income during the period 1857–74 ran to about 55 per cent.

The institutions of mid morning coffee and afternoon tea that had hitherto been preserves of the leisured classes in the eighteenth century were now rapidly being adopted by the new middle class. To these institutions perhaps a third, late evening period might be added in which Huntley and Palmer's biscuits might well have been consumed with Cadbury's cocoa and chocolate as a late repast designed to head off 'night starvation'.

Certainly Huntley and Palmers had a close knowledge of their customers' tastes. In 1849 they introduced a biscuit called the Pic-Nic which proved such a winner that the factory had to work 24 hours a day to keep up with demand. Two years later it accounted for 20 per cent of all the company's sales.

The English custom of morning coffee and afternoon tea was really a result of the decline in the consumption of large breakfasts or hot three-course lunches. With husbands travelling some distance to their work as a result of the development of the suburbs and their associated railway system, there was no longer such a need for cooked lunches and with that went a reduction in the activities of wives left at home. Thus at both the office and in the home alternative snacks were being sought. Huntley and Palmers went out of their way to cater for this rising demand and a whole string of today's household brand names were being poured out of the Reading factory.

Among their customers were the Earl of Radnell, Viscount Sidmouth, the Earl of Rosse, Lord Willoughby de Eresby, Mrs Hawtree, the wife of the headmaster at Eton, the principals of King's College, Cambridge and Exeter College, Oxford, the Bishop of Carlisle, and the Bishop of Lincoln, and finally the Royal family itself. The example set by the Royal family led Napoleon III of France and Leopold II of the Belgians also to appoint royal warrants to the firm of Huntley and Palmers.

It was not only in the home that the new consumer patterns involving so much biscuit eating were established. Up and down the country that other great English institution, the tea shop, was springing up. Until the end of the century there were a whole range of restaurants and tea shops where customers were demanding factory-produced biscuits and cakes with their pots of tea.

The development of road and rail communications had by the second half of the nineteenth century created the concept of long-distance travel. As people began increasingly to go on long train journeys they became aware of their discomfort at the lack of dining facilities. Restaurant cars on railways were not to appear until the end of the century. In the meantime travellers comforted themselves with biscuits, chocolate and cakes which were carried in tin boxes. These were purchased at home before the traveller left or, indeed, on the stations. The Palmer brothers who had always travelled far and wide in the development of their business were well aware of the inadequate refreshment facilities, so much so that every first-class passenger departing from Paddington was handed a small packet of biscuits in a neat wrapper with the instructions to look out for Huntley and Palmer's works at Reading. It was and indeed is still a conspicuous landmark close to the railway on entering the town from the London side. Thus it was that Huntley and Palmers established a marketing practice that is used to this day in hotels, on ships, and by airlines.

By 1860 Huntley and Palmers were the largest biscuits firm in England producing 3,200 tons of biscuits and turning over £180,000 a year. The Company was acknowledged to be the leader in the industry. The scattered baking shops of thirty and forty years before had been replaced by an industry with a recognizable shape. Other firms had grown up as well as Huntley and Palmers to cater for the new market. In particular we find Carr's of Carlisle who had Quaker connections. Another competitor to Huntley and Palmers, whose name today is also a household word, was the new firm of Peek Frean and Co. in London. Having been formed in 1857, they were by 1862 in partnership with the Quaker John Carr who was the younger brother of the founder of the Carlisle firm. In this century they were to become associated with Huntley and Palmers through the establishment of the Associated Biscuit Manufacturers Ltd.

With Huntley and Palmers of Reading it may be seen at the end of the period of partnership of the three Palmer brothers that once again the expansion of the works was to bring about a development of the company's activities. In 1873 new building of what became known as the North Manufacturing Department was opened. These premises not only included manufacturing and packing facilities but also involved the construction of railway sidings that would run into the heart of the factory. This gave the Department its own loading sheds into which cases of biscuits were passed from packing rooms on the upper floor down inclined planes. The company was even to have its own locomotives that hauled the waggons to and from the main London to Reading railway lines to which the sidings were connected. The cost of these buildings was around £75,000.

The partners ceremoniously declared the buildings open in November 1873. The company now numbered 2,500 employees and altogether some 4,000 were invited to the opening. Married men brought their wives or another member of the family. Unmarried men with over five years' service were allowed to bring a female member of their families. We may suppose that this was a classic Victorian euphemism since we can be certain that some of the young men's partners were extremely distant relatives indeed.

The guests were served with refreshments including the Company's biscuits. Then they were given a choice of no less than eight entertainments for the rest of the evening. These varied from scientific and travel lectures to displays of clairvoyance, juggling and comical sketches with titles such as 'Pussy's Road to Ruin'. There was also a band which played music for the dancing of quadrilles, waltzes and polkas. The proceedings closed with the entire company standing to sing the National Anthem. Four months later George Palmer's sons, George, William and Alfred, were admitted to partnership and a new phase in the management of Huntley and Palmers of Reading was begun.

The three Palmer brothers were bound closely together by a strong sense of duty inherited from their mother, Mary Palmer. This sense of duty was born of a feeling of responsibility to their own superior intelligence and hardworking habits. George was concerned with adult education. He sat on the committee of the Mechanics Institution and as his responsibilities for the day-to-day running of the factory increased, he became more committed to serving the community. He became secretary of the boys' school in Southampton Street, Reading. This had been founded in 1810 on the pattern laid down by the great Quaker educationalist, Joseph Lancaster. He put a lot of work into this school, building up a strong committee of management and being closely concerned with its day-to-day operation. He also went into politics and was attracted like so many other Quakers to Liberalism with its strong nonconformist and temperance element. It is clear that he could be counted amongst the more radical members of the Reading Liberal party. He was elected to the town council and, like the Cadburys in Birmingham, was wholly concerned with civic affairs during a time of enormous expansion for the town. He was interested in public hygiene and, in particular, with a general drainage bill which Reading Corporation presented to Parliament and also the 1848 Public Health Act. He finally allowed his name to go forward as Mayor for the year beginning November 1857.

He lived eventually in a modest villa of Bath stone, called Saltbox Hall, in the London Road. Today it forms the nucleus of the University of Reading. He also owned nearly 2,000 acres of land in Berkshire, Hampshire, Oxford and Surrey, which he rented out. He lived a rather austere, middle-class life in this suburb of Reading. He continued to acquire land to become quite important as a landowner in Berkshire, and was elected to Parliament in 1878 as a Liberal. With the shift of political power from the old landed proprietors to businessmen, it was increasingly common for entrepreneurs such as Palmer to become MPs. He decided to go into Parliament as a result of a personal appeal from a true Quaker in high places, John Bright, the former Cabinet Minister. Throughout his period in Parliament he exhibited a rugged refusal to seek personal or social advancement. He took a town house in Grosvenor Street, halfway between Paddington Station and the House of Commons. He did not get along too easily with the London Friends and in a sense he could have been said to be exhibiting the typical provincial nonconformist face that was also very much part of the style of many Quaker entrepreneurs. His life in London brought an inevitable compromise to the rather more austere tenets of his faith exhibited at Reading.

Of William there is less to say. He, too, became a substantial landowner but took a more active interest in agricultural activities. His shorthorn herd was one of the finest in the country and he carried off many prizes. He too was a philanthropist who quietly and without thought of reward spent a great deal of money on good work. He was, for a long time, one of the central figures in the temperance movement in England. He supported at his own cost a free library in Reading and gave £25,000 to the municipal library and reading room in the town.

William never married, taking the responsibility of looking after his elderly mother as the only member of the family really able to do so, and he consistently declined all invitations to enter public life. He seems to have been a thoroughgoing professional, and created single handed the London office which not only developed sales in the London area but also overseas.

Samuel gave the business an international standing and he was a true cosmopolitan. He married in 1856, at the age of thirty-six, the daughter of one of the Company's agents who was also related to the Clark family. It is interesting that they ceased to be Quakers during their marriage and like many other entrepreneurs found that the Church of England provided a more acceptable framework for their life-style and attitudes. Samuel seems to have exhibited all the features of a home-loving, domesticated businessman, but he also enjoyed an excellent business and social reputation throughout the City of London. Towards the end of 1887 he fell sick with rheumatism and never fully resumed work, although he was to live for another sixteen years, outlasting his two brothers and surviving into the early years of this century.

The Company went into the last quarter of the nineteenth century as one of the major individual industrial enterprises of the nation. The total output of the Company was now very close to £1 million per annum, and it was responsible for a half of one per cent of the total exports of the United Kingdom at a time when its overseas trading was at its greatest. The Company was then employing some 3,000 people.

The last quarter of the ninteenth century was marked by a relative economic recession for the United Kingdom. From the 1870s other countries, notably the United States and Germany, were beginning to match Britain's early industrialization and to take advantage of mechanical improvements. As they developed into serious competitors for Britain, the physical volume – but more especially the unit value – of British exports was falling markedly, and this had its effect on Huntley and Palmers, whose exports during this period dropped from 36 per cent per annum increase to one of only 11½ per cent. Deliveries to the Continent in particular were affected and the growth rate of 61 per cent per annum towards the end of the previous period was not matched, falling to a steady 10 per cent.

The management of Huntley and Palmers was undergoing a change at this time. From 1874 onwards a new generation of the Palmer family was coming into partnership after undergoing suitable apprenticeships. George Palmer's two eldest boys, George William and Alfred had joined the firm as unpaid clerks at the age of sixteen as soon as they left school in 1868 and 1869 respectively. They were given a thorough grounding in every part of the factory, and plenty of time to learn their trade; indeed their father did not seem particularly anxious to give them any real financial independence and throughout their apprenticeship they had to be content with a modest allowance. Before finally deciding to make the boys partners in the firm, even after reaching the age of twenty-one, George Palmer sent them to

Vienna for the International Exhibition. Their work on the firm's display there was regarded as a sort of final test of their ability. They passed with flying colours and received a personal congratulation from the Prince of Wales. They were admitted as partners from the beginning of the financial year that commenced in the last quarter of the century, 1874–5.

Four years later Ernest Palmer, Samuel's eldest son, was admitted to the partnership, and George's third son, Walter, became a partner a year later. Over the following twelve years, they were to be joined by three other sons of Samuel Palmer – Charles, Howard and Albert. All these young men were taken into partnership some time after their twenty-first birthday, having served at least three years' apprentice-ship. The only exception was Walter Palmer whose training included a B.Sc. degree from London University.

Naturally, the two fathers, George and Samuel, tended to encourage their sons in their own particular areas of interest. Ernest and Charles were trained in the work of the London office whereas Howard and Albert Palmer concentrated on the work at Reading. During this period the partnership arrangements remained representative of the two fathers – George Palmer and his two sons owned one half of the shares and Samuel Palmer and his four sons owned the other half. It was also during this period that Huntley and Palmers ceased to be the traditional Quaker family enterprise. Like so many other Quaker families they found themselves unable to reconcile their wealth and status with the demands of the Society of Friends.

George and his partner, the founders of Huntley and Palmers, had all the motivation and enterprise to take advantage of a time when all kinds of experiments were possible. Success created a different con-cept of business for the next generation. They had grown up within the confines of a successful enterprise, and did not feel themselves to be so alienated from the social establishment as their fathers had. George and Samuel Palmer had gone to a Quaker school that prepared boys for commercial careers; they sent their sons to middle-class schools and their sons, in turn, went to Eton or Harrow and up to Oxford. George and Samuel had lived fairly modestly in proportion to their wealth; all but one of their sons had country estates and pursuits. This social transformation inevitably coloured their attitude towards the business, local societies, and also the Establishment, all but one of the second generation joining the Church of England, which pro-vided at that time a more comfortable religious ethic in which the entrepreneur could operate. All but one of the second generation rejected the Liberal Party in favour of the Conservatives.

The first generation finally disappeared from the Company during the 1880s. In 1887 Samuel Palmer, the partner who had established the London office and the overseas trade and purchasing network, began to fail in health. His two elder sons who had for some years been assisting him took over the London office completely. Samuel's third son was at Reading where he held a key position in overall charge of the manufacturing and packing department. His youngest son, Albert, was responsible for tins, labels, showcards and miscellaneous publicity.

Meanwhile, the sons of George Palmer were equally well esconced in the business. George Palmer's eldest son (also called George) was responsible for the administration of the Company, while Alfred was in charge of the engineering department which manufactured the biscuit machinery and some of the dynamos and boilers. The generating engines were touchingly named after his wife, Alice, his daughter Phyllis and his granddaughter, Betty, respectively. Walter, another son, was an able working scientist who created the firm's scientific department, and travelled round international exhibitions scrutinizing very carefully the products and ideas of rival exhibitors. His greatest triumph was to discover the breakfast biscuit. It proved an immediate success as a substitute for the baker's roll which in high circles was usually consumed with early morning tea or coffee.

Despite the fact that this new generation, wealthy, and socially comfortable, was moving away from the austere spirit of their fathers, they remained very much a family unit. In the main they kept free of outside business commitments – although Ernest Palmer's directorship of the Great Western Railway was entirely in keeping with the habits of members of other Quaker families of the time – and they tended to be clanish and inward looking and most anxious to maintain entire control in their own hands.

One of the great strengths of the Quaker connection, however, had been the interrelationships that resulted from a large family. Apart from making good marriages with other businesses, the members of a family – were it sufficiently large – could comfortably control all the aspects of the business. As an enterprise increased in size, it was necessary to produce more and more children to manage it. Unfortunately, in the case of the Palmers the reverse had happened. The eight sons of George and Samuel Palmer had no more than seven sons altogether, and of these only five were to enter the business. This meant not only that their administrative ability would be stretched to the utmost but also that as private venture capitalists their financial resources were inadequate to meet the demands of a growing business. As with the Lloyds, Huntley and Palmers were ultimately affected by the various Acts of 1856–62 which had authorized the setting up of joint stock companies. Huntley and Palmers had been owned entirely by the three brothers of the first generation and the second of the second generation. The partnership, even after the passing of the Joint Stock Acts, still remained the predominant form of business organization in British commerce, the mid-Victorian world commending the idea of families taking the whole of their private fortunes into their own businesses. But by the 1880s the joint stock company was beginning to make headway. The nominal capital of new companies registered between 1873 and 1888 had nearly trebled to £353,000,000. Increasing taxes on inherited wealth and death duties were also draining off private wealth which previously had gone into the business. Huntley and Palmers, like the Lloyds, were in no particular hurry to go public and follow the example of other biscuit manufacturers. Jacobs Biscuits of Dublin had gone public in 1883, Carr and Co. Ltd in 1894, and Meredith and Drew in 1891.

Although in 1894 the firm's Quaker accountants, Price Waterhouse, were requested by the Act of Parliament to investigate the possibility of converting the business into a joint stock company, it does not seem that this was any more than good housekeeping by the enterprise. Clearly they would wish to look at all possibilities for the future of the firm but one feels that as long as George Palmer, the founder, was still alive decisions involving radical changes in the structure of the operation were likely to be deferred.

About a year after William Palmer's sudden death in 1893, George Palmer's wife, Elizabeth, also died. She had been a good wife to him and had played her part not only in providing him with a stable domestic environment in which to conduct his life and bring up his children but had also apparently been active in social welfare in the town of Reading. George, who by this time had little to do with the business, now became subject to fits of depression. His eyesight began to deteriorate and he wished to spend as much time as possible with his children and grandchildren.

At the beginning of 1896 George Palmer proposed to retire from the end of March. However, brother Samuel in London, whom we recall was also suffering from diseases of old age, deplored the idea of his retirement. The whole family should, he said, present a united front to the world; moreover George and he could allow nature to end their connections and thus free themselves from the criticism of those who would be surprised at the action of George's resignation so late in his life.

George Palmer put off his decision to retire, accepting Samuel's argument that nature should take its course. The following summer he suffered a severe stroke but he was soon able to go out again for short periods. He was to live for another year, dying on 21 August 1897 only a few months short of his eightieth birthday. He was buried in a simple grave alongside Elizabeth Palmer in the Friends' burial ground at Reading. The grave is only a few feet from where Thomas Huntley and his wife and his own mother, sister and youngest brother lay.

With George Palmer's death the surviving partners immediately went ahead with preparations for creating a limited company. These preparations did not take long, for on 29 March 1898, Huntley and Palmers Limited was formally incorporated. Samuel Palmer took the opportunity of this reorganization to mark his formal retirement. At the beginning of the twentieth century, the second generation of Huntley and Palmer was finally and totally in control, given the context of a limited liability company, and it was to be fifty years before the last survivor of the second generation finally severed his connections with the firm. The Company was capitalized at £2,400,000, £1,000,000 in ordinary shares and £1,400,000 in 4 per cent preference shares. This was divided equally between the two branches of the family with George Palmer's three sons on one side and Samuel Palmer's four sons on the other.

They joined the large number of limited liability ventures of the time that remained essentially family partnerships. The Articles of Association of the Company made it clear that members wishing to sell their shares should offer them first to their own side of the family and then to the other. This apparent contradiction led to an Act of 1907 effectively distinguishing between the public company, whose shares are offered to the general public, and the private company. This distinction remains to this day, dividing companies offered on the Stock Exchange from those that are not.

The incorporation of the Company represented a definable staging post from the independent enterprise of 1842 and the corporate giant of today. In 1844 there were seventeen employees who earned on average 11s. 3d. per week. By 1904 there were 4,857 employees earning an average of 19s. 7d. per week. Today the average is over £40 a week. In 1841 the turnover was £2,700, by 1904 it had reached £1,400,000, and today approaches £10,000,000. Finally, the known output of the Company has risen from nearly 3,000 tons in 1859 to 37,447 tons in 1968.

Undoubtedly the most important change in Huntley and Palmers organization after incorporation as a limited liability company was the establishment of the Associated Biscuit Manufacturers Limited during the period 1919–29. In 1919 the Company decided that it should become a public company, and that approaches should be made to the other leading biscuit manufacturers of the day on the subject of a possible amalgamation. The decision to go public led to a move by the junior directors of the business for a complete reorganization of the management structure of the venture. This was carried out over the following year to the Company's ultimate advantage. Meanwhile, Harold Palmer, the chairman, had kept open negotiations with other firms, particularly with Peek Frean, and at a special board meeting at the end of 1920 he obtained his colleagues' unanimous agreement to start informal talks with the object of a merger with them. Arthur Carr, the chairman of Peek Frean, and a cousin of the Carrs of the Carr biscuit company in Carlisle, warmly welcomed the approach. The two existing companies were to become subsidiaries of a new holding company. They exchanged their ordinary shares for those of the holding company on the basis recommended by their accountants. Fifty-two and a half per cent went to Huntley and Palmers and the remaining 47½ per cent to Peek Frean. Of the authorized capital for the holding company of £2,500,000, just over £1,000,000 went to Huntley and Palmers and £850,000 to Peak Frean. The remaining £500,000 was put up for cash subscriptions to meet the expenses of formation. The Associated Biscuit Manufacturers Ltd was incorporated on 1 December 1921. Everybody concerned took great pains to deny that Peek Frean had in any way been taken over by Huntley and Palmer. Howard Palmer was elected the first chairman and Arthur Carr became the vice-chairman, and the managing directors of the two companies became joint managing directors of Associated Biscuits. About this time negotiations began with Jacobs Biscuits of Ireland for them to join the enterprise. It was to be 1950 before this actually took place. The growth in development of Associated Biscuits Ltd during the twentieth century is part of the general development of British enterprise in this century and as such constitutes another story.

In 1960 W. R. Jacob and Co. (Liverpool) Ltd became a wholly owned subsidiary of the Associated Biscuit Manufacturers Ltd. It simply exchanged its shares for group ones. The group thereby increased its issued share capital to £7,200,000. Three of Jacob's directors joined the group board and Roderic O'Conor, a grandson of one of the firm's original partners, became a joint managing director together with Gordon Palmer and Rupert Carr. The group was thus fortified by the accession of a quality firm having a nationwide sales network in a complementary line of biscuits. To add to Huntley and Palmer's and Peek Frean's well-known specialities, the brand name of Jacob's Cream Crackers and Chocolate Varieties were added. Turnover in 1960 rose as a result to £31,600,000, an increase of £7 million pounds over the previous year. The diverse interests of the units of this group, were ultimately self-contradictory and again a degree of reorganization and rationalization was necessary. This was carried out as a result of recommendations from independent consultants, the group headquarters being moved to Reading as part of the reorganization.

As the newly electrified trains today pull out of Reading station on the way to London, the factories and plant of Huntley and Palmers still dominate the southern aspect of the town. It is still a major employer in a town that is rapidly developing modern industrial enterprises in the electronics and construction fields. Associated Biscuits Ltd stands as one of the three giants that dominate this section of the British economy and for all its connections and partnerships, the memory within that enterprise remains that of its earliest founders, Huntley and Palmer, while the principal site of the enterprise remains in Reading where it was first begun more than 150 years ago.

CHAPTER 8

The Rowntrees of York

In 1977 Rowntree Mackintosh declared that during the previous year their turnover had amounted to almost £385 million, of which their profit came to about £37 million. A list of their products provides a virtual inventory of the shelves of any supermarket or store selling confectionery and groceries, including a whole range of well-known brand names from Black Magic to Sunpat (peanut butter), KitKat to PanYan (pickles), Aero to Cremola. The same would be true of similar stores in Australia, Canada and South Africa, while Rowntree Mackintosh, through these famous names, is penetrating the confectionery markets of France, Germany and the other EEC countries.

The origin of the Rowntree Mackintosh story goes back to the end of the seventeenth century. York, like Bristol, Birmingham and Manchester was a non-corporate town having a high degree of religious tolerance, so much so that Quakers such as William Tuke were able to be Freemen of the city. In 1693 William Tuke, who was by trade a blacksmith, married Rebecca Smith of Thirsk. They had several children, the survivors being Mary and Samuel. William Tuke died in 1704 and in 1723 the children lost their mother. Thus Mary and Samuel were left to fend for themselves without family connections to draw on. As blacksmith's children they were not wealthy and although Samuel had begun to carry on business as a stuff weaver, he did not earn enough to sustain their household. Mary, by this time thirty years of age, and unmarried, determined to go into business on her own account.

Apart from being a Quaker and a woman, Mary Tuke had a number of things against her. It was necessary for a prospective merchant to become a Freeman of the city and this could only be done by purchase, through apprenticeship, or through having a relative who was a Freeman. Women were granted such status as the wives of deceased members. Although Mary could not put forward this qualification, she was able to quote her father as a member, and was inscribed in 1725 on the Freemen's Roll of the City of York as 'Maria Tuke, spinster Fil Willelmi Tuke, blacksmith'.

This distinction was not sufficient to allow her to trade. It was necessary, in addition to being a Freeman, to be a member of the York Merchant Adventurers' Company or to be licensed by that body to trade. Mary Tuke had no grounds on which she could apply for such a licence so she decided to start trading and take the consequences, attempting to break down a system which had ceased to be useful and which was based on custom rather than reason. As a result she was prosecuted on 28 June 1725 at the Midsummer Court for selling groceries. The Court was prepared to excuse her if she gave an undertaking to give up trading, but having started she had no intention of doing so. For two years she continued to defy the Company and at the end of that time she was given six months to dispose of her goods. Nine months later she was given liberty to trade until the following Lady Day Court when she would have to pay a fine of £50 or be prosecuted.

Fortunately, compromise was in the air and in July 1728 the Company began to show signs of yielding and Mary Tuke was given liberty to trade at the pleasure of the Court, provided she paid five shillings to the wardens of the Company every six months and bought all her goods in the city. Four years later it was resolved that she should have the liberty to trade during her life on payment of the sum of £10.

In 1731 Mary's brother Samuel married Ann Ward of Drumfield, Derby, and their son, William, was born a year later. He was admitted in 1746 to an apprenticeship in the service of his aunt Mary, who by this time was a widow. He was her favourite nephew, largely as a result of his hard-working nature and his kind attentions to her when she became an invalid, and in 1752 she left him her shop in Castlegate and other property. After some hesitation he decided to carry on the business by himself and in 1753, a year in which he also married Elizabeth Hoyland who came from Sheffield, he took up his freedom of the city as a grocer; in the following year on the termination of the period of his apprenticeship he was duly admitted to membership in the Merchant Adventurers' Company. Life was hard for him and for several years the business showed little sign of achieving any success, and it was not until his eldest son, Henry, who was born in 1755, joined him in partnership that the situation changed.

When Henry was recalled to York in 1785 to join his father he had taken up the study of medicine, wishing to become a doctor. The fact is interesting not so much because he abandoned medicine to assist in the establishment of the family business but because it throws a sidelight on his father's activities as a Quaker. For over a century the intelligence and reason of the Quakers had led them to take a more enlightened attitude towards the insane. Lunacy was still regarded as a crime and those bereft of reason were not treated as invalids but at best as prisoners. The shortest method of keeping a madman quiet was to knock him down and chain him up. Tuke opened an establishment in 1796 at which the methods of looking after mentally deranged persons were entirely different. He considered not the ease of the keeper but the interests of the patients who were to be kept in order by kindness while unnecessary restraint and discipline were to be avoided. This was The Retreat in York. It attracted attention all over the civilized world and it was to be the foundation of the modern treatment of the insane. Although this was still to come, in 1785 we may be certain that William's interests in these affairs had created a continuing influence on Henry's desire to become a doctor.

Henry was made a partner in the business in 1785 and notwithstanding his scientific training, he proved to be a most valuable asset to the growing concern, and it may be said that the Tuke family's prosperity dates from this period. Under Henry's management a small cocoa and chocolate factory was established which became the nucleus of a commanding concern. 'Tukes' Rich Cocoa', 'Tukes' Plain Chocolate' and 'Tukes' Milk Chocolate' were among the brand offered for sale. (Milk chocolate gained its name, not because it contained milk, but because it was for mixing with milk as a drink.) They also sold at a charge of one shilling per pound 'British Cocoa Coffee', a mixture of cocoa and coffee, chocolate at 2s. 3d. and cocoa nibs at 1s. 10d.

Henry brought to the business that essential Quaker combination for success. In addition to hard work and no little sense of enterprise he had been well educated and had a wide knowledge of scientific matters which would have assisted him in the development of his products. He was also an important figure in the Society of Friends and an author whose books became standard interpretations of Quakerism.

His son, Samuel, entered the firm in 1805, thus creating a partnership in which there were members of three generations of the Tuke family. Samuel remained head of the firm for nearly half a century till 1852, and like the third generation of other Quaker families who had achieved a successful enterprise, he was able to extend himself in a number of directions. He was active in politics and did his utmost for the return of William Wilberforce as a member for the County of York. He also took an active interest in his grandfather's retreat for the insane.

He also established the Friends' Provident Institution in 1832, known today as the Friends' Provident and Century Life Office. It was in following these interests that he spent a considerable amount of time with his friend Joseph Rowntree. Together in 1829 they founded the Bootham School for Boys, a landmark in the history of Quaker education.

In 1849 William Tuke decided to transfer his tea business, started in 1835, to London and in 1860 he relinquished their cocoa and chocolate department to the ownership of its manager, Henry Isaac Rowntree. Thus for the first time the name Rowntree appeared in a cocoa business that was to become as well known as Cadburys. Henry Isaac, born in 1838, was the youngest of three boys born within four years of each other. Joseph, who was to become the great force of Rowntrees, was two years older and John Stephenson, born in 1834, was the eldest. The Rowntrees had been Quakers for several generations. The boys' father, also called Joseph, had bought a shop in 1822 on his twenty-first birthday. He, and a friend called James Backhouse, acquired the property at an auction at an inn in York. The auctioneer was drunk but the two men buried his head in a bucket of water and managed to sober him up enough to conduct his business. Thus 28 Pavement, York, became Joseph Rowntree's property.

Everything was rather dilapidated but the building itself was a graceful Georgian structure with two bow windows and a fan light over the shop door. Joseph put the new house in order and got his business off the ground. He had the advantage of ten years' experience of the grocery trade, as his father had owned a grocer's shop in Scarborough and he had left school at eleven to work in it. It had not been a very flourishing business which was the reason why Joseph had gone to York on assuming his majority.

Everyone worked very hard in the new shop which was open from six in the morning to eight at night on six days of the week. There was no early closing day and the only holidays were Good Friday and Christmas Day. The Pavement shop never had a serious setback in its affairs and as the years went by the elder Joseph employed more and more young men and many additions and alterations were made to the shop. In 1832 he married Sarah Stephenson from Manchester and two years later she gave birth to the first of the three boys.

The Rowntrees were very active in the Society of Friends and frequently brought members of the Society together in simple gatherings at their home. Sarah often found it necessary to cook for attenders at the quarterly meeting of the Society in York. There was also evidence that she travelled on behalf of the Society to investigate refractory Friends and to help and console those in trouble. The children were given a good education at home and although Bible readings after breakfast were a part of the daily routine, it was by no means a solemn house. The boys were given joiners' tools and encouraged to make collections of plants. They also carried out simple chemical experiments, such as the manufacture of gas by using a small coal placed in the bowl of a tobacco pipe and covered with putty. When this was placed in the fire a small stream of gas issued out of the mouthpiece of the pipe. They also enjoyed making electro-types of casts made of plaster of Paris and took gelatine impressions from coins. They had a governess but were never separate from the large mixed household. The boys also learnt to take a share in their parents' affairs and had a fairly detailed knowledge of everything that went on in the shop.

The family stayed in the shop-house until 1845 by which time two girls had been born. In that year they moved to a house in Blossom Street, just outside the city walls. The boys were sent to the Friends' School in York and their habits of wearing plain country Quaker dress brought them a certain amount of teasing from their colleagues. It seems that the boys enjoyed their time at school and were considered good pupils. Towards the end of their time at school they were taken to Ireland by their father and spent a year there.

On leaving school the two older boys, John and Joseph, went into the Pavement shop working as apprentices for their father. The fact that they were related to the owner of the business made no difference to the way they were treated. They obeyed the same rules and did the same jobs as the other young men. The rules had been very carefully thought out and survive in a memorandum, which the older Joseph wrote in 1852, intended to serve as a guide to new employees. The following extracts indicate that the guide was, in fact, almost a classic recipe for a Quaker business.

> *The object of the Pavement establishment is business.* The young men who enter it . . . are engaged to assist in this business . . . to contribute their part in making it successful. The arrangement . . . affords full opportunity to any painstaking intelligent young man to obtain a good practical acquaintance with the tea and grocery trades, including the purchasing of stocks and the keeping of books. Access is freely allowed to invoices, accounts of sales, cost price of articles, etc. . . . . It should be understood that the value of the situation . . . mainly depends on the temper and disposition of mind of those who enter it. It presents good opportunity for the industrious to learn but there is little direct business teaching. The place is not suitable for the indolent and wayward. . . . Punctuality in the time of rising is important in each member . . . the thoughtless or ease-loving individual wastes the time of the others . . . much time is unavoidably occupied with meals. . . . much may be done by

consideration and arrangement to prevent the needless extension of mealtaking. . . . It is very desirable that these occasions of meeting together should be of a social and uniting character . . . every morning . . . each man records in a book . . . the exact time at which he enters . . . a gratuity of 26 shillings per year is allowed to the punctual. The household may in all respects maintain all those habits and practices in regard to dress, language, which distinguish the religious Society of Friends.

The young Rowntree boys learnt that the trade of grocer involved a great deal of skill and discernment if business was to prosper. They learnt how to blend and grade China and Indian teas; to distinguish between grades of butter and cheese; to purchase flour and to test the great hogs' heads of Demerara and Barbados sugar. They learnt that the grocer's goods carried his own name as a guarantee of satisfaction and that his reputation was a personal one. They also learnt standards in working that they were to carry, almost fanatically, with them into their later life.

In 1855 Henry Isaac and Joseph went with their father to London to attend the yearly meeting of the Society of Friends, and for the first time the boys were introduced to the leaders of the Society of the time, among them the Radical John Bright. They were also introduced to the City. Joseph Rowntree, the younger brother, in particular, went back to York with his mind full of the sights and sounds of London. He persuaded his father to let him live and work in London and in 1857 he was established there in lodgings, working at a wholesale grocer's in the City, where he remained until the death of his father in 1859.

The elder Joseph had become a successful and well-known man of York. The mayor and corporation followed the funeral procession to the Friends' burial ground and all the shops in Pavement were closed as a sign of respect. Joseph must have died feeling that his work had been done and leaving very few loose ends behind him. His campaigns within the Society of Friends over the marriage regulations, which hitherto had precluded Friends from marrying outside of the Society, had been successful. The boys' school in York which he had helped to establish was flourishing, and a girls' school had also been established. His sons were making their way in life and his widow was comfortably settled in a good house. It was no small achievement for the young man who had come to York when he was twenty-one with little capital except his ability, industry and integrity.

The whole management of the Pavement grocery business now devolved upon the sons, but it is not clear why Henry Isaac was not given part of the business and why it devolved instead on young Joseph who was twenty-three, and his elder brother, John, who was twenty-five. They were reasonably well off but there was not a great deal of money to spare. What we do know is that a year after his father's death, Henry Isaac went to work for the Tuke cocoa business. Probably Henry had obtained some sort of financial gain from his father's estate because certainly in 1862, only two years later, he was in a position to buy for himself the Tukes' cocoa and chocolate making department.

The change of business was announced as follows:

> We have to inform you that we have relinquished the manufacture of cocoa, chocolate and chicory in favour of our friend, H. I. Rowntree, who has been for some time practically engaged on the concern, and whose knowledge of the business in its several departments enables us with confidence to recommend him to the notice of our connections.
> We remain very respectfully
> Tuke and Company
> York. 1st of seventh month 1862.

A circular was enclosed with this announcement and in it Henry Isaac informed his customers that he was prepared to execute any orders with which he might be favoured. He inherited a brand of cocoa that was much esteemed in the neighbourhood of York – 'Tukes' Superior Rock Cocoa'. It sold for ninepence a pound and was a blend of pure cocoa and sugar compressed into a sort of cake. This cocoa was subsequently renamed Rowntrees Prize Medal Rock Cocoa, and was the main product of the factory for which Henry Isaac had become responsible. Excellent though Prize Medal Rock Cocoa was, Henry Isaac could not make enough profit out of it to finance the extension of his business. In the year 1862, for example, his total sales were estimated as being under £3,000. He invested in a new machine for grinding cocoa and also a collection of buildings for which he paid £1,000. These buildings were an old iron foundry, several cottages, and a tavern, all close together down by the river. On one side ran the little street called Tanners' Moat and it was by this name that Henry Isaac's factory came to be known when he moved from the original premises in Castlegate.

It was a tiny enterprise employing less than twelve men and having an output of about twelve hundredweight of cocoa per week. For the first seven years Henry Isaac had a hard struggle to keep the business going and he found himself in a position of some difficulty. This, however, was resolved when his brother Joseph took his capital out of the Pavement shop and put it into the business at Tanners' Moat. The Rowntrees understood the concept of family responsibility and it was this that led Joseph to learn a new trade when he was already thirty-three years old. He took over the accounting side of the business and left Henry Isaac to deal with the actual manufacture of the cocoa. Joseph really understood figures for as part of his campaigning for the Society of Friends he had mastered statistics of national expenditure on the problem of pauperism and now he began to apply some of this expertise to the unit costs of producing various brands of cocoa. He carried out this activity with a high degree of accuracy and meticulous attention to detail, adopting a scientific approach to every problem to the ultimate advantage of the business.

Tanners' Moat in those early days was little more than an eighteenth-century workshop. There was a parrot in one of the work-rooms and a temperamental donkey in the stables who was given a Turkish bath from time to time by means of steam pipes run from the factory. The donkey could only be handled by one attendant, and he kicked everyone else so fiercely that eventually he had to be sold, making it necessary to do local deliveries by hand cart. Cocoa and pork pies were provided by Joseph and Henry Isaac Rowntree on nights when men had to work overtime, and wet coats were dried on hot pipes in the roasting department. Joseph had a private office with an end window overlooking Lendel Bridge. He had a trap-door in the floor beside his desk and if he wished to speak to anyone in the counting house below, he pulled up the trap door and called the man's name. Urgent letters for the post were also dropped through the trap-door with the request that someone should take them over the bridge to the Post Office.

The situation at Tanners' Moat was typical of the circumstances in which Quaker enterprises were developed. The entrepreneurs knew all their employees and regarded them as part of their family. No one at Tanners' Moat in those early years could fall ill or run into any sort of domestic or financial trouble without Joseph or Henry Isaac hearing something about it. As there was no system of state insurance against unemployment, sickness or old age, such concerns were to a large extent dependent upon the character and the capability of an employer to provide safeguards. The Rowntree brothers were very conscious of the tradition in which they were reared and had a reputation for looking after their work people. In return they got good service and the kind of loyal interest which is perhaps only possible in a small concern where each individual is aware of his own part in creating the end product.

It was another ten years after Joseph's arrival before they made any real commercial progress. This may have been due, in part, to a general trade depression, for prices fell steadily from 1873 to 1879. Both English farming and industries were beginning to feel the effect of foreign competition. It is interesting to note that it was not until

1875, on the birth certificate of his third child, that Joseph ceased to describe himself as a master grocer in favour of the appellation 'cocoa manufacturer'. Rock Cocoa continued to be the mainstay of the business but the firm also manufactured Iceland Moss Cocoa, Chocolate Powder, Hexagon Cocoa, Pearl Cocoa, Flake Cocoa, Farinaceous Cocoa, Chocolate Creams, Shilling Chocolate, Confectionery Chocolate, Shield Chocolate, Chocolate Drops, and Halfpenny and Penny Balls. They also had one or two side-lines such as an early fruit sauce composed of a granular effervescent citrate of magnesia and they were the local agency for the sale of Neaves' Farinaceous Food for infants.

Part of the problem lay in Joseph's opposition to advertisements of any kind and the only publicity in the early days was supplied by rather restrained letters to wholesalers. Joseph's opposition to advertising seemed to be based on his Quaker instincts of truth telling and he was vehemently opposed to anything which savoured of an unsubstantiated claim for the quality of any of his firm's products.

They initiated a system of selling cocoa to shops to be retailed under the shops' own name, much as larger supermarkets today obtain similar supplies for marketing under their own brand names. Rowntree and Co. also supplied the labels for this type of customer which were sent when they delivered the cocoa. Joseph Rowntree on at least one occasion wrote an outspoken letter condemning in no uncertain terms the wording of one such own-named label. He said: 'I extremely dislike the wording of this label and will be no party to supplying a new man with a similar one. It is not a pure ground cocoa. It is not produced from the finest Trinidad nuts. It is not the best for family use. In fact, the whole thing is a sham, not to be creditable to anyone concerned with it.'

The Rowntrees trusted to the quality of the goods they sold to make their own impression on the public. They had grown up in a grocery business that operated on the notion that it was a well-stocked shop that was more important than goods in the shop window. They knew their cocoa was good and they thought that it would sell on its merits. In the 1870s, however, they put themselves at a considerable disadvantage at a time when advertising had begun to be a factor in commercial success. There were also certain technical handicaps which resulted from the smallness of their operation. All the chocolate was made by a staff of seven, who took turns in grinding, roasting, rubbing and fetching in the sugar. They had only two small machines to do the mixing of the chocolate and eight hundredweight was a very good day's output. The chocolate cream department was started by a foreman, named Hanks, with one girl as his assistant, though in addition it seems he also acted as nightwatchman for he lived next door to the factory. He was also the wages clerk. Wages at this time for a man averaged around 15s. to 18s. a week at most. In addition they had two clerks in the office and two desks. Money in general was tight for the Company and did not allow the possibility of expansion. So it was that by 1873 the business at Tanners' Moat, in spite of increased sales, had shown a loss of £500.

Meanwhile in Birmingham the Quaker Cadbury brothers had installed a Dutch machine which extracted the fat from the cocoa beans by hydraulic pressure. What remained was cocoa very much as it is known today – a light powder which can be sold unblended with sugar or anything else. Joseph Rowntree paid a visit to Birmingham in 1875 and also two short visits to Holland eighteen months later. He also spent his holidays in 1877 in Switzerland with the Cadburys and we may be certain that much of the Rowntrees' technical and financial problems would have been the subject of earnest discussions with his friends. Although it was a long time before the Rowntrees came to invest in such machinery, their interest in experimentation was obviously quickened, for in 1879 Claude Gaget, a Frenchman, called upon the Rowntrees with a sample of the gums which he had made. Until this time gums and pastilles were made almost exclusively by the French. No firm in England had yet produced anything to compare with the imports and the Rowntrees decided to try their hand.

Crystallized Gum Pastilles went on sale early in 1881. They were sold loose in four-pound wooden boxes and were available at one penny per ounce. The pastilles were an immediate success, and within four years the firm was employing twice as many people. Profits were no longer modest and the Rowntrees were now to look towards the development of their enterprise.

The year 1883 was not a good year at a personal level for the family. Both a nephew and two nieces contracted typhoid whilst on holiday in the country, but the death that affected Joseph most was that of his brother, Henry Isaac, in May. It seems that he had a sudden attack of appendicitis causing death by peritonitis. Only forty-five when he died, Henry Isaac left a widow and three young children. It was unfortunate for Joseph that he was left on his own at a time when trade began to be difficult again. Prices were falling and once again the accounts began to show that the firm was making a loss. Previous short-lived success had encouraged the Company to buy land at a place called Foss Islands which they had never used, and also a flour mill in North Street adjoining Tanners' Moat where they urgently needed more space for the manufacture of their gums. All this had cost money and in 1883 some £12,000 of the Company's capital existed in the form of mortgages and bank overdrafts. The interest was a heavy drain on the small factory struggling to keep going through a general slump.

The depression deepened during the period 1883–6. In every area of industry production fell considerably and things were so bad that by 1886 a Royal Commission was appointed to enquire into the depression of trade. Towards the end of that period, Joseph's sons, John Wilhelm and Seebohm – named after his mother's family – entered the business. They were not formally apprenticed but were sent to every department of the factory to become thoroughly acquainted with the practical side of the work. They stayed long enough in each workroom to understand all the various processes, achieving good relationships with the other employees and learning a great deal about the necessity for good industrial relations.

They found a factory still in that first stage of improvisation. There were some 200 employees and more space was constantly needed. The flour mill in North Street had been altered and several additional storeys of workrooms had been built above Joseph's office. There remained only two coke-fire roasters for the cocoa beans and there was no mechanical method for getting them on and off the fires. There was one carpenter and one engineer possessing a hand hammer, a coal chisel, and one or two fires. The firm was now producing somewhere in the region of a hundred different lines. The boiling pans were turning out four tons of gums and pastilles every week and by 1887 a flat horse-drawn lorry was needed every day to take the factory's output to the station.

The good years after 1886 saved the business. Every year Joseph would buy some new property or refurbish the old. More offices were added to the flour mill and eventually in 1888 some small houses next door were replaced by six storeys of workrooms. At last the business was making money, a process no doubt assisted by a change of heart on the part of Joseph towards the necessity for advertising. The inherent dignity of Quakers, as reflected in their advertisements, remained an attractive selling point to the Victorian middle classes of the 1880s.

Joseph took advantage of his fact-finding trips to Holland and engaged a Dutchman called Cornelius Hollander, installing him in rooms at the top of the old flour mill and fitting an iron door with a padlock to the entrance of this apartment. The result was 'Elect Cocoa', which began to compete almost at once with the older forms of cocoa. It was the modern product, a powder from which the surplus fat had been extracted and not requiring the addition of sugar before being placed on sale. The name 'Elect' had been taken from an expression used in the druggists' trade to describe quality. It was first put on the market in 1887 in a year in which prices were rising and it thus had a good start. The period from 1875 to 1886 is regarded in British social history as one of great depression but it was the Rowntrees' good fortune, or Quaker sense of timing, to launch their gums and their cocoa during short periods when trade was on the upturn and they were able to exploit a rising market.

The result of this and further expansions meant a growth in the size of the Company from a staff of 200 to one of 894. With so many employees it was no longer possible for Joseph to know every single person, his problems and ambitions, nor to maintain the paternalistic system that had been possible in the early years of the Company. Neither was it possible to communicate through heads of departments to groups of specialists with common sets of values and ambitions. At this time the pattern was for individual men to make their way upwards through various departments, much as the messenger boy at a film studios may end up many years later as a producer or senior cameraman. A business such as Rowntrees in the 1880s could no longer depend upon the capacities of the 'Master'; it had become too large and too valuable for that to be the case. It was therefore necessary to work out a less precarious system of industrial management: something that would survive the changes and chances of a single man's life. The responsibility for making this change lay in the very hands of those who had grown up under the paternalistic system and who in most cases were not broad minded enough to understand the economic consequences of not doing so.

It was a period of exploitation and indifference on the part of the masters to the problems of their workforces. To many of them labour was just a factor of production, something to be bought and sold according to market forces. They lacked the enlightenment of the Quakers in understanding that such relationships were not only immoral but ultimately economically self destructive. Joseph understood this and although he remained autocratic in practice, he was something of a benevolent dictator. Like the Cadburys, he sought ways of improving the environment of his workforce, both industrial and cultural. In 1885, he started a library; books, mainly suitable for young people, were bought, and one penny per week was arbitrarily deducted from the wages of every single employee for the library's upkeep. In view of the fact that average earnings at the time were still only about £1 such a deduction was substantial. There is no evidence of anyone objecting to the deduction, but whether this was the result of an enlightened understanding on the part of the workforce of something that was for their own good or whether it amounted to a Victorian acceptance of the rights of masters to do as they pleased, it is not possible to tell.

In the world of late nineteenth-century industry such benevolence, even though it may have been authoritarian, was unusual. Most employers felt bound only by the safety and sanitary conditions that had been imposed through legislation in 1875. They felt that if they kept to the regulations they were doing all that was expected of them. Joseph Rowntree was part of a very small group of businessmen who managed their firms in a more enlightened way.

Despite Rowntree's attempts to develop the literary tastes of the employees, the root of good employer–employee relations lies not in the external or peripheral benefits that may be provided but in the actual conditions of work itself. The factory at Tanners' Moat was unprepossessing and as a result of its piecemeal development it was not a satisfactory working place. He was also aware that his employees often came from slum domestic conditions. It was not possible for him to do much about the objective conditions of work at Tanners' Moat but he took the unusual step in 1891 of appointing a woman to take charge of the girls' health and behaviour. Such an appointment was a revolutionary one and this first welfare worker at Rowntrees held the position of a pioneer. She demanded that black dresses be worn at work by the girls, blouses and skirts being forbidden, as were embroidery trimmings and coloured frocks. A year later an assistant welfare worker was engaged. The first woman had by then proved her worth and so many little odd jobs had been handed over to her that she could not cope with them on her own. She ran the lending library, she dealt with girls who fell ill, investigated absentees, helped to arrange social festivities, and was at the beck and call of everyone with a decision to make or a problem to solve.

A less satisfactory experiment in social welfare was an outing for which a special train was engaged to take the firm's work people to the sea. The plan was that those who wished to do so could leave the train and walk across the moors to Whitby where they would rejoin the others in the afternoon for a walk on the beach. The party that left the train to cross the moors got soaked to the skin and instead of going to the beach they went to warm and welcoming public houses, and whilst their clothes steamed by the fire the workers of Joseph Rowntree proceeded to become unmistakably drunk. The police even had to escort them to the train. Joseph was obviously shaken by the outcome of his scheme and for many years there were no further outings.

He continued to arrange occasional festivities for the whole firm, such as concerts at a local exhibition building. Tables were laid with a substantial meal and there were recitations as well as music. For the poorer workers who could afford very little entertainment such gatherings were extremely popular. The office staff were also invited to social evenings at Joseph's own house. He still interviewed personally all new applicants for an office job and by this time the office staff were no longer required to take off their coats and help move sacks of sugar and cocoa. The office was a congenial place in which to work, but the long hours and the rigorous Quaker demands on accuracy and precision were quite tiring.

After 1886 the business never encountered any real setbacks, and by 1890 turnover amounted to £110,000. In Joseph's eyes the factory at Tanners' Moat no longer absorbed his interest. The semi-domestic arrangements for his employees that had sufficed in 1880 were no longer appropriate ten years later. He was anxious to practise, like so many of the Friends, his scientific approaches to production but he had no scope to do so. At first he considered the possibility of expanding on the Tanners' Moat site as indeed he held land in the adjacent streets, but like the Cadburys, he decided in the end on a clean break. In 1890 he bought 29 acres of land in Hacksby Road on the outskirts of the city. Like the Cadburys he was going to build a new factory, large, light and properly equipped, which would give him the opportunity not only to try out new technical developments in the manufacturing and processing of chocolate and cocoa but also allow him to experiment with the social and working conditions of his employees. His aim in his own words was to make it easier for men and women to develop all that is best and most worthy in themselves.

It is worth digressing for a moment to look at Joseph Rowntree's domestic arrangements at this time. His beloved mother, Sarah Rowntree, who had come with his father to open the Pavement shop at York, had died but two years before. Joseph and his wife, Julia, purchased a house and moved in. In another part of the house his brother's widow and her three children were also established. The house came to be known within the family as Top House and was one of a number of Rowntree establishments in the neighbourhood. Within ten years two of Joseph's sons and one of his nephews had also set up house in the district which was known as St Marys. Joseph, now over fifty, he still had thick dark hair and a beard. He was a thin man, energetic and quick moving with bright blue eyes. His financial worries were over and his children were growing up to his satisfaction. John Wilhelm, his son, had not only done well at the factory but was also an active member of the Society. Both witty and perceptive in his comments on the Society's practices, he once described them as 'Quaker caution and love of detail run to seed'. He was also a serious writer and yet as an individual was known for his fun and gaiety.

The Top House was a place full of Quaker traditions. The sons lived very similar lives to those of the third generation of other Quaker families. John Wilhelm travelled abroad, Seebohm studied economics at Manchester, and Stephen went up to Cambridge. There was good food in the house, well-cared-for furniture, fine linen, many books and a few pictures. Their lives all displayed a typical Quaker combination of wealth and lack of ostentation. There was also evidence in the family of scholarship which owed more to independent thinking than to any university training.

The building of the new factory at Hacksby Road began fairly quickly. Joseph was determined not to carry over to the new factory the problems that were beginning to develop at the old. He was anxious to achieve a balance in the relationship between himself and his employees and also inculcate a positive attitude towards their jobs on the part of the employees. These were tasks that could be begun at Tanners' Moat for, without either problem being satisfactorily resolved, the new venture would be less likely to succeed.

The men who had grown up with the firm, who could remember the bosses in their shirtsleeves, who had perhaps worked at three or four different jobs, were in a minority. Having this personal identification with the business they were unlikely to lack interest as they watched it grow and develop. But they were increasingly outnumbered by girls of thirteen or fourteen who came to the works straight from school. The girls spent long hours in the factory and would look forward to their evening out with well frizzed hair and a bright frock. Yet their lack of earning power really prevented genuine evening entertainment. The girls lived in a restricted world in which pregnancy and early marriage was all too frequent.

Joseph was aware of these problems and of the fact that most of their life was spent in his factory. He was anxious to discover what job satisfaction they were obtaining and if indeed they even liked their jobs. He wondered about the relationship that existed between his workers and whether they were in any way of assistance to each other during the long hours of the day. Joseph, who looked at people and their requirements against a set of positive fundamental values, was able to determine some of the answers to the problem, and he was fortunate that his two elder sons, who had both been made partners in the firm on achieving their majority, were capable and willing interpreters of his ideas. There was also Arnold, a son of Joseph's brother John, and Henry Isaac's son, Frank. All the young Rowntrees were influenced by Joseph and his ideas and brought to them the advantages of their own upbringing and education. They had the advantage also of being close to the ground in terms of their relationships within the factory.

One of the most revolutionary schemes to be discussed at this time was the establishment of a pension scheme open to all employees. Four thousand people were employed by Rowntrees when the pension scheme was finally set up in 1906. Nearly everyone was working at Hacksby Road by that time and the last of the old workrooms of Tanners' Moat was about to be closed. No one regretted leaving the old factory as it had never been a congenial workplace, but it had seen the greater part of the early development of the Rowntrees.

The new factory was not beautiful by modern standards. There was one very high chimney surrounded by low blocks of buildings. The departments were moved one by one, beginning with the fruit room and the gum-making department. In 1897 the new offices were ready and they were the first part of the works to be lit by electricity. The factory used its own generating plant to supply not only light but power. The place was an efficient unit and like so many Quaker concerns it had its own branch railway line. Production increased quite substantially as a result of the move, and in the five years between 1894 and 1899 the number of Rowntrees employees was again doubled. This, of course, is a phenomenal rate of growth by today's standards. It had never been Rowntree's intention that his cocoa works should grow so large but once the process had been set in train it was difficult to stop and he was too good a businessman deliberately to check it.

In 1897 Rowntrees became a limited liability company and changed its name from H. I. Rowntree and Company to Rowntree and Company Limited. Joseph was the first chairman of the board and the other directors were his sons, John Wilhelm and Seebohm, his two nephews, Arnold and Frank, and J. Bowes-Morrell. Arnold's brother, Theodore, was appointed secretary. The addition to the board of these sons and nephews was important not only because they guaranteed the maintenance of Rowntrees Ltd as a family concern but also because they provided the essential continuity between generations that was so important in Quaker companies. Joseph depended a great deal on his sons and relatives, inculcating in them his own code of ethics but at the same time listening attentively to their young and often progressive ideas.

The continuity was threatened in at least one case when in 1899 it was necessary for John Wilhelm to leave the factory. Although he was only thirty-one, he was not strong enough for daily work and was going blind. The blindness was a devastating sentence for one who was already deaf but apparently he accepted it with great courage. He went on working at Rowntrees as long as he could but the moment came when he had to retire from the business. He went to live in the country, though he continued to be a director and still kept a finger on some of the firm's social activities.

Social activities as a means of improving relations within the Company were now a fact of life at Rowntrees. There were organized clubs and societies for readings, concerts and social evenings. There was a cricket club, singing classes, dressmaking classes, an angling society, and bowling, camera, cycling, football and tennis clubs.

Meetings were also held to discuss poetry and novels and sometimes to read plays. The firm was growing at a rapid pace and there were plenty of employees to take part in these activities.

Trade was good and their new ventures into advertising helped the firm to make the most of the favourable times. The Elect Cocoa staff, for instance, had grown from six men to a department employing 240 people on a permanent basis. Its weekly output had increased from 16 cwt to 26 tons. The story was similar in other parts of the factory. The original joiner now had two foremen and a staff of thirty-seven.

Joseph was approaching seventy. He had been in business for over fifty years and seen a radical change in its shape. Gone was the medieval tradition of obedience to a master, gone was the subjection of children and powerless adults in the mills, gone too was the individual's interest in a small enterprise. He now had 3,000 people in his factory and could have only little contact with the majority of them. But his sense of responsibility remained and he tried to find practical answers to the problems created by the size of the Company. He found welfare workers useful as a way of keeping in contact with the individual problems of his employees, and he gave much careful consideration to the work and the workers of particular departments and also to the personality of the men who might be in charge. Departments were now becoming units of their own and there was less coming and going between them; even workshops in the same building often had little contact with each other. Joseph feared that the close and comfortable relationships that grew up between individuals engaged in a common task might be lost in the increasing size of the business.

In 1902 he started the *Cocoa Works Magazine* in a deliberate attempt to close some of the gaps. His concern can be seen in some words of that first issue: 'The increasing numbers of those who are associated with the cocoa works makes it impossible to keep up a personal acquaintance with the staff . . . if the business is to accomplish all that the directors desire in combining social progress with commercial success, the entire body of workers must be animated by a common aim . . .'

There were very few house journals in England at this time and those who did introduce them generally confined themselves to articles of technical interest, statements on production in different departments, and stories from commercial travellers. The *Cocoa Works Magazine* broke new ground. It was well printed on good paper, there was a good deal of topical factory news in it. Activities of clubs and societies were regularly reported and staff deaths, marriages and promotions had their place. There were also cultural reviews and articles, photographs, poems and parodies.

Rowntree used the magazine to develop yet another idea. This was the suggestions scheme, an innovation in the industrial world of the time. Suggestions were invited for improved methods of manufacturing, packing or in the quality of goods, for quicker or more economical methods, for improvements in machinery, for improvement in working conditions, and on any other matter that might affect the welfare of the Company or its employees. Prizes were offered for the best suggestions actually adopted. The suggestions scheme had a slow start but eventually grew to become a regular feature of the Company's existence.

Joseph had one other great vision – a vision with strong parallels to that of Cadbury Brothers in Birmingham. He enjoyed village life and saw a contrast with life in his own city of York. His son, Seebohm, had published a book on urban life, showing that York's housing situation was certainly in need of improvement. Over 10 per cent of the population were living in back-to-back houses often built round airless courtyards. There were slum areas which were said by experts to be filthier than any in London. Even the more respectable houses inhabited by the working class were not very inspiring and were well on the way to becoming slums. They had no gardens although occasionally there was a small railed-in front lawn.

In 1901 Joseph bought 123 acres bordering the land already owned by Rowntree and Co. This was the beginning of the village now called New Earswick. Several projects of this kind had already been started, among them those of the Cadburys at Bournville, of the Quaker, Sir James Reckitt, at Hull, and Sir George Lever's village for his employees at Port Sunlight. It could be argued that the idea of building accommodation for the workforce was simply a continuation of the days of tied cottages but it is necessary to be more charitable. People like Rowntrees, the Cadburys and Reckitt were moved far more by their aversion to the violent, depressing working and living conditions of their work people than they were by any other motive.

New Earswick was something of a risk. York was a city of few industries and it remained to be seen whether Earswick would be able to pay its way. The estate was not designed as a philanthropic enterprise, nor was it intended that the cottages should be let only to those employed by the firm. Joseph's ambition was to provide well-built sanitary houses of artistic appearance yet within the means of men earning about 25s. per week. It was a challenge to the prevailing bad housing and building, but to be effective it had to make a return that was less than that at which local authorities could borrow from the public works' loans board, which meant less than $3\frac{1}{2}$ per cent on average.

In the first three years thirty houses were built and let at approximately 5s. per week. Unfortunately, it was discovered later that 6s. 1d. was the minimum that would have to be charged for cottages of this type. The trustees accepted the fact that they would have to reduce their standards if they were to provide anything in the range of the lowest paid workers with whom Joseph was most concerned. As a result a cottage was designed without a bathroom or hot water supply that could be built for £135 and let at 4s. 6d. It was at least an economic proposition even if less than ideal. The houses had as tenants artisans, shop assistants, and clerks, but all persons who earned their living wholly or partly by the work of their hands or their minds were eligible for them. Joseph was anxious to create a mixed community such as might be found in any ordinary village in the country. The land was flat and uninteresting and in the early days there were no trees to disguise the newness of the site, nor were there buses or street lights, while the roads were rough and full of pot-holes. Although the New Earswick houses were invariably far better than those in the city at a comparable rent, at the outset it was only a limited number of families who were prepared to move into them while the village was still in its infancy.

Today the village has changed substantially. Additional land has been bought and accommodation provided for people with very varied requirements. There are large numbers of three-bedroomed houses on the estate as well as flats suitable for single people. There are both primary and secondary schools, a small hostel for old people, and a large community centre. Playing fields and sports grounds have been enlarged and a nursery school established for children between the ages of two and five. Modernization has taken place over the years, the roads have been metalled and trees planted to lend a far more attractive aspect to the estate.

In many directions Joseph's hopes were realized. The village became a real community of the kind that he had in mind. Earswick has indeed contributed much to the conception of a neighbourhood unit in large urban areas. The fact that it developed into such a community remains a tribute to the vision of Joseph Rowntree who understood that communities were about people and not just bricks and mortar.

Joseph's eldest son, John, died of pneumonia in America in 1905. Joseph and his son had been very close to each other and held many things in common. The boy had worked in the business whilst it was still small and struggling, and had lived in the first house that Joseph had after his marriage. He had also stood strongly beside his father in the Society of Friends. Most important, perhaps, was that he had been a man of gaiety and wit. This was something that his father had prized above all and it must have been a sore loss to him when his son died. It must also have turned Joseph's mind to thoughts of his own death. The problem of what to do with his money lay heavily on his mind for he was afraid of its effect on his family. His income had been increasing yearly and income tax stood at 8d. in the pound. He was not interested in luxuries and what extravagances he did go in for were few in number. He also disapproved of the type of benevolence that gave or willed thousands of pounds for the construction of hospitals and sanatoria, feeling that such institutions were the responsibility of the state and not that of private charity. At the same time he saw the inheritance of his money by his children as likely to have a permanent effect on them.

He knew the advantages that he had gained from his own strenuous childhood where in the house above the Pavement shop there had never been much money. It was a pattern that Joseph admired. As a result he decided to give one half of his property to the establishment of three trusts. The first was established as a social, charitable and religious trust to finance social surveys, adult education and the activities of the Society of Friends. The second was a social trust with the power to undertake social and political work which could not be legally supported by funds belonging to a charitable trust. The third was the village trust which was concerned with living conditions and, in particular, with the houses at New Earswick.

These trusts remain famous to this day and many a leading politician, including recent prime ministers, have been grateful for the addition of one or two extra research workers paid for by grants from the Rowntree Trust. Equally the welfare trust remains active, particularly in key areas of health and care; it has been involved more than once in controversies over the causes it has sought to support.

Joseph wrote a memorandum for his trustees which he thought might be helpful. His aim was to indicate what had been in his mind when he had created the trusts. He felt that charity as it was understood at the time was worse than useless. Much of our effort, he said, is directed to remedying the more superficial manifestations of weakness or evil. Little thought or effort is directed to search out their underlying causes. It is always easier to obtain funds for famine-stricken areas than to finance a survey on the causes of famine. Soup kitchens in Victorian England were never short of funds or willing workers from the upper and middle classes. It was more difficult to obtain adequate financial aid to support an enquiry into the extent and causes of the poverty that created a need for the kitchens in the first place.

Joseph's attitude was fomed as much by his connection with the Society of Friends as by his own independent and original thinking. It is likely that he saw problems in his dual role as Quaker and businessman but the principle of prevention rather than cure was very much the philosophy of the entire Society of Friends. Money was not to be given except in special circumstances towards the building of meeting houses, adult schools, or social clubs. The need for such buildings was so obvious that the money was certain to be supplied. The Quaker disdain for overt philanthropy included their continued contempt towards the attitudes of Church and State. Privilege was still the order of the day and no amount of donating of monies gained through privilege could alter the fact that the way in which it was obtained was immoral. The greatest danger to the country, in Joseph's eyes, was the power of selfish and unscrupulous wealth. It influenced public opinion, sought only its own ends, and countenanced every form of international social division, opium traffic, the liquor trade and the South African War.

In 1905 Joseph chose a house for his retirement and like his father he moved a little further away from the city. This was Clifton Lodge, originally a Regency dwelling with a sitting room on either side of the front door and a drawing and dining room off the far end of the hall. He also acquired several acres of land and a couple of cottages. He built shelves for his large library and installed some of the furniture from his old house at St Marys. He continued to live as he had always done, devoting the daytime to his business and his spare time to his political activities, his welfare committees, and his family.

Joseph Rowntree was also interested in the development of newspapers designed for the mass reader. The Education Act of 1870 had produced a generation of ordinary people who were able to read and write, and this produced a great change in the newspaper world. Following the publication of *Titbits* and *Answers*, both of which were different from what they are today, the *Daily Mail* was started in 1896 and the *Daily Mirror* in 1904. These were aimed specifically at the mass market, were smaller in size than newspapers such as *The Times* and cost half the price. As far as content was concerned, they were less interested in the great political affairs that would dominate the older newspapers and concentrated on items of mass social interest. The traditional newspapers, both national and provincial, had had no photographs in them and few sensational headlines. This sober treatment was now challenged by the new newspapers. The sensational dailies grew in circulation every month, flooding the country on a tide of jingoistic sentimentality, and were captured by financial interests that were both warmongering and anti-liberal. They were able to whip up national feeling in favour of the Boer War. Another feature that did not endear them to Quakers was the fact that they carried extensive encouragement of gambling in the form of printed racecards with 'tips' and betting forecasts.

Joseph, in his memorandum to his Trustees, mentioned the possibility of the Social Service Trust controlling a newspaper if funds permitted and the Trustees felt equal to the task. Not long after the Trust was established such an opportunity presented itself. The manager of the *Northern Echo* approached Joseph for financial help in starting a York and North Riding edition of the paper. Joseph had other ideas and suggested that the Social Service Trust should acquire control of the whole paper and his suggestion was accepted. This was the beginning of the Trust's interest in newspapers and led in the course of time to the association now known as Westminster Press Provincial Newspapers Limited, which went on to control no less than sixteen newspaper companies.

The *Northern Echo* was intended to counter the shallowness and superficiality of the national dailies. Joseph's nephew was the first chairman of the group of newspapers controlled by the Trust and Mr Bowes-Morrell, who had been on the original board of Rowntree & Co. Ltd, was one of the first directors. They applied the great Quaker principles to their enterprise: it had to be established on a sound financial basis and become self financing, though it was not necessary to make a large profit. The papers existed to serve the community with information of local interest and also to be of service in a moral sense in trying to point a way to a more healthy and fulfilling life.

By the end of 1905 York like the rest of the country was suffering from a recession and unemployment was high. The end of the Boer War had brought an end to the war economy and trade was bad. Prices had risen faster than wages, and at the same time employers' profits were increasing. The inevitable result was an outbreak of strikes in 1910 and 1911. Rowntree and Co. remained generally unaffected by this general discontent, and Joseph decided to embark on some building operations partly in order to provide work for some of the unemployed in York. He was troubled as ever by the divisions in society and particularly by the ostentation of the Edwardian middle classes in the face of working-class poverty and unemployment. Anxious as he was to keep up his employment in the works he was not satisfied that the employment of welfare workers to help with domestic situations was sufficient.

He was also aware that ill health was another factor which plagued the workers and in 1904 Rowntree and Co. followed the lead of Cadbury Bros. by appointing a doctor for their employees – his son-in-law, Peter Macdonald, who had married his elder daughter. Dr Macdonald soon discovered that a major cause of ill health among the employees was bad teeth and so the Company appointed a dentist to provide free services as well. 'Healthful conditions of labour are not luxuries to be adopted or dispensed with at will,' said Joseph Rowntree, 'they are conditions necessary for success. In keen international competition the vigour and intelligence of the workmen are likely to be a determining factor.'

Joseph, believing that factory life did not fit a girl for home duties because she never had the time or the opportunities for learning how to manage a home, then established a domestic school with a staff of teachers. Girls who entered the works before they were seventeen were now obliged to attend the school's cookery classes. These took up two hours every week but the girls' time was paid for by the firm so they lost no money. In 1907 a course in Swedish physical training was established for boys, and a few years later continuation classes consisting of maths, English and woodwork were begun. These, too, were compulsory for any boy coming to Rowntrees before his seventeenth birthday and four hours of the firm's time were given up to it. Joseph was certain that in commerce and industry a lively educated mind was more essential than anything else.

The Company continued with its innovations. In 1906 there were nearly 4,000 people employed together at the works. Joseph was aware that the old, the young and the sick made up the majority of those in poverty and so in 1904 he appointed a committee to examine the question of a pension fund. It was a revolutionary idea and one which took a long time to work out. It was still only thirty-five years since Joseph had first gone to work with Henry Isaac at Tanners' Moat. Some of the men who had started with him at that time were still not yet old men. Had they begun at the usual starting age of thirteen they would still be in their early forties at this time. Perhaps it was these men, who had little chance of saving anything in the subsequent twenty years of their working lives, who concerned Joseph most. Perhaps it was the contrast he felt between his own secure impending retirement and those of his workers which prompted him. Either way he aimed to establish a pension equal to at least half the wage a man was earning when he retired. Subscription tables were designed to provide minimum pensions of 15s a week rising to £1 if the member's wage was more than £2 per week. The contributions were to vary with age being at least 2½ per cent of wages and maximally 5 per cent. The Company was to pay into pension fund one and a half times the amount paid by men and three times that paid by women.

The firm rather than the insurance company underwrote the pension fund. This was a serious financial undertaking and a large sum of money had to be set aside for the purpose. It was hoped that the cost to the firm would be no more than 2½ per cent of the total wages and salaries bill.

Joseph gave £10,000 of his own money to the fund when it was first set up and the Company contributed about £9,000. These sums allowed the fund to operate on a solvent basis from the start and meant that people could start drawing pensions as soon as the scheme was in operation.

The scheme was so well thought out that in many ways it has remained a model for similar schemes. The firm decided, for instance, that pensions should be linked to inflation – in those days simply called 'money value' – and that the pensions should also be kept in step with wages. The fund had exceptionally wide investment powers and this was to benefit the fund enormously. Ninety-eight per cent of all those employees who were eligible joined it in its first year.

The fund was also called upon towards the end of the 1914–18 War to assist widows of men who had worked for Rowntrees and had been killed in the war. Joseph pressed for the establishment of Widows' Benefit Fund which under certain conditions would provide pensions for widows who were aged fifty or more at the time of their husband's death. Joseph was clearly a perceptive man in so many ways but despite all his efforts to supply social and moral support to his workers, he understood that their prime interest lay in the money that they were earning. He wrote in a private memorandum, 'I have no doubt that as the intelligence and self-control of the workers increase claims will be made for the share of profit which comes to labour to be increased while the share which comes to capital is lessened.' Although he felt that they were right in establishing a pension fund, health and education facilities, and a minimum rate of wages, he saw all these things as only the first steps. He argued that the directors of the Company at some time would have to address themselves to the problem of a profit sharing or co-operative scheme.

Profit sharing as an idea had been around in one form or another for sixty odd years. The idea of co-partnership often aroused fear and resentment. The managers felt it wrong that their workers should have any measure of control in the company which employed them, either by acquiring share capital or by setting up committees of workers who would have a voice in the internal management of the factory. The trade unions on the other hand were unanimously hostile and such people as the Webbs described profit sharing as a disastrous undermining of the solidarity of the working class. What they and trade unionists really meant was that their very existence and ability to negotiate depended upon the consciouness on the part of working people of a division between themselves and the owners of capital. If this distinction were to be blurred through co-ownership, then it was felt that the workers would be exploited through their own greed and the great causes of labour would be lost. Joseph's notions therefore were not very popular, but he was a shrewd man who understood the necessity of waiting till the right time to introduce his ideas.

Apart from arousing the political ire of the Conservative Party for his association with the Cadburys in the purchase of the *Star* and the *Daily News*, Joseph Rowntree made few personal enemies. He was made an honorary Freeman of the City of York in May 1911. This was the highest honour within the power of the city and only twenty-three names appear on the honorary Freemen's Roll from 1876 to 1911. Furthermore, Joseph was the first man of business to receive this honour, the others being drawn from the aristocracy, the military, the Church or the professions. The mayor and council attired in their robes made speeches of welcome, reviewing Joseph's achievements at the cocoa works, the establishment of the model village at New Earswick and the many generous contributions he had made to the life of the city. Joseph replied by outlining the growth of York as he had known it in his lifetime, praising the improvements and public health and education and the reform of municipal elections. Towards the end of his speech he turned to an area of thought which stood out against the polite phrases and graceful compliments. He referred to the poverty that would follow when the breadwinner of the family was ill. He outlined in detail the events that normally followed such calamities and asked what street was there in the working-class districts of York in which these tragedies had not been known. It was a challenge to a company of prosperous people and he was lifting the corner of the civic cloth to reveal to those present the reality behind it.

In the remaining years of his life, from 1911 to 1925, Joseph remained physically active, mentally alert, emotionally calm and thoughtful. It was the period when the Indian summer of the Edwardian era came to an end followed by the outbreak of the War. And yet before the War industrial strife was developing and Joseph was aware of the dockers' and seamens' strikes in Goole and in Hull, which took place in 1911 to the accompaniment of rioting crowds of men and women who raged through the streets smashing and destroying whatever they could lay their hands on. From other parts of England, from Lancashire, Wales, Southampton and Manchester, there were similar stories. Fear was a common feature throughout the land and almost every resident in England was kept ready for action. Strikes raised a spirit of violence in factories and workshops all over the country that was the very antithesis of everything that Joseph himself believed and had worked for.

The cocoa works had no staff troubles at this period, and there is no hint of discontent in the Company magazine of the time. Out at the model village in New Earswick more houses were being built, a folk hall and a football club started, and the village council was finding its feet and beginning to agitate about education. These were not the issues that bedevilled other communities up and down the country. The 1914–18 War was naturally a distressing time for the pacifist Joseph as he watched with sorrow the destruction of many of his hopes of international peace. Members of his family were killed to add a personal element to his sadness.

To the end of his life Joseph maintained his enthusiasm and intellectual curiosity. He had as a result of his long experience formed some very clear ideas about the way in which business should be done and we may see that these ideas were, as usual, eminently practical. He insisted that there had to be trust between employers and employees and that this trust had to be a two-way process. This was achieved through several quite radical practices. Once a year after the chairman of the board had given his usual address to the shareholders another meeting was held. It was open to all the employees and a comprehensive survey of the previous year's activity was given to the workers, with the request that it was to be regarded as confidential. There is no evidence that this trust was ever abused by a single worker.

Another arrangement was the establishment of works' councils, each consisting of equal numbers of administrative staff, appointed by the management, and workers elected by ballot amongst themselves. They were regarded generally with suspicion by the trade unions who feared their own authority might be undermined, but the reason why works councils have come to be accepted throughout the country and union fears allayed was through the example of those at Rowntrees.

Throughout the history of the Company – apart from the General Strike of 1876 – there have been only two strikes of a minor character and very short duration. In 1919 when the works' councils were asked to help in a revision of the works' rules which had been drawn up a long time previously and without consultation with the employees at the time. A vote was taken of the entire works on the rearrangement of hours that resulted in the factory being closed all day on Saturday. This was done in exchange for working longer hours during the week. It was a very popular move, as was the decision to grant all factory workers a week's holiday with pay every year – a very unusual practice at this time and nineteen years before the principle was enshrined in an Act of Parliament. Unusual also, was the decision to give each workroom a voice in the appointment of its foreman or forewoman.

A small committee from each department was asked to give their opinion on the individual nominated by the management. If they approved of the appointment the matter was settled. If they disapproved of it they were required to suggest someone else, and his or her appointment was then discussed by a joint committee of management and workers. Although the directors reserved the right to have the final word, in the first fifteen years of the scheme it was recorded that they had never needed to exercise their rights. This exists to this day in a modified form where the management makes a nomination and consults the appropriate steward before the appointment is made.

Joseph and his son, Seebohm, worked closely together throughout this period. In 1916 Joseph returned once again to talking about profit sharing, to find his directors no more enthusiastic than they had been previously. But he persisted, writing a memorandum in which he said that he challenged those who held that a profit-sharing scheme was not applicable to a business like Rowntrees. He argued that if no form of collective profit sharing was possible, how could the directors ensure that an intelligent interest in the prosperity of the business would be taken by the workers? There were many arguments both from the directors and from the trade unions who reasoned that the profit sharing was an attempt to weaken their power by individual bargaining between single firms and employees. He listened also to the patronizing comments about the inability of working-class people to manage their affairs and that if they were dependent upon profits then in a bad year they would run into debt. Joseph and Seebohm finally got their way. When Rowntrees' directors had considered an independent report by William Wallace on the real reasons for the success or failure of other schemes, they decided to adopt the principle of profit sharing, and a scheme was put into force in 1923. It was extremely popular with the workers and although it was slow in getting off the ground, very few profits being distributed in the early years, their patience was rewarded and in the period from 1943 to 1953 no less than £1½ million was distributed.

At the same time as the introduction of the profit-sharing scheme, the Appeals Committee began functioning successfully within the Company. It was a unique example of a court of justice being set up within an individual enterprise and it brought to the world of industry the principle that everybody had the right to be tried by an impartial tribunal.

The Committee was composed of five people; two were elected by the workers, two were nominated by the directors and a chairman. Any employee who felt that some disciplinary action was unjust could appeal to this Committee. It had powers either to confirm the original decision or to reduce or increase the penalties which the management had imposed. Authority depends on justice, Seebohm said. When a wrong judgement is made there should be the machinery available to correct it. This was the purpose of the Appeal Committee which at the time was so strange and revolutionary. And yet it was the same principle of open democracy and justice that prevailed at the Pavement shop a hundred years earlier when the staff was small enough for everyone to know everything that was going on and therefore to be in a position to discuss it. Today the concept of an Appeal Committee is inherent in many major commercial and industrial enterprises and certainly in every local authority.

Joseph's wife died in November 1924, five days after the fifty-seventh anniversary of their marriage. In February of the following year Joseph was writing at his office in the works when he complained of feeling cold. He was persuaded to go home to bed and he did not see his beloved cocoa works again. He died five days later in the early afternoon of 24 February.

His legacy is both to his city and to the whole world of industry. He was a fine example of the great Quaker ethic and his monuments were the tree-lined roads at New Earswick, the public swimming bath he had given to the city, the public park and playing fields that had been the company's memorial to the staff who died in the First World War. His memorial is also the development of fair and just industrial relations and an effective company operation. He had shown the world of big business that labour was as important a factor in business as capital, but also that the human element needed to be dealt with humanely. Joseph himself would not see his life as being noble or sentimental. He saw justice as a practical necessity and his ideas and developments were for him a matter of expediency. He believed in prevention rather than cure.

CHAPTER 9

Allen and Hanburys of London

Following George Fox's decision in 1647 to seek his own way to the truth and to battle for it, it was but seven years before the first Meeting of Friends took place in London.

It happened in the back room of the 'Bull and Mouth' in Aldersgate. At that time the City was not only the business centre but also the main residential centre of London. The tradesman lived above his shop, the money-man above his counting house and the physician among his patients. With their preference for trade, and for banking, and their progressive scientific instincts the Friends established themselves in all three.

In 1715, Sylvanus Bevan set up shop as a druggist at No. 2 Plough Court, off Lombard Street. He was twenty-four, and came of Welsh Quaker stock. The family were from Glamorgan – Sylvanus's great-grandfather having Anglicized the family name from Jenkin-Ap Evan, to Bevan. Sylvanus's grandfather William Bevan had joined the Society of Friends, giving up his position of alderman of Swansea at the same time. William Bevan had founded the Quaker meeting house in Swansea and his grandson had grown up in a staunch family of Friends.

In 1709 Sylvanus went off, like so many other young Friends, to become apprenticed to an apothecary, Thomas Mayleigh. The completion of his apprenticeship was marked by his admission to membership of the Society of Apothecaries in 1715 and by his having to pay a fine of £6 9d. in place of serving out the rest of the agreed apprenticeship time.

Sylvanus was a young man in a hurry. In 1715 he leased the premises for his pharmacy from Salem Osgood, a Quaker merchant, and in the same year successfully courted and married Elizabeth

Quare. She was the daughter of Daniel Quare who was, by Royal appointment, clockmaker to George I. They married at the Friends' meeting-house in Gracechurch Street with over one hundred witnesses, including a large party from Court circles.

The Society of Apothecaries had been established a hundred years before, the trade having evolved from that of grocery. The grocers in turn had evolved from peppery. The Guild of Pepperers went back at least as far as 1180 when they allied with the Guild of Spicers. Thus today's chemist owes his origins to the wooden ships that brought back peppers from foreign parts for the merchants of London. As the importers widened their wholesale activities they became grocers (who at that time were not retailers). In addition to selling peppers and spices, the grocers dealt in herbs and drugs.

It seemed logical, therefore, when the assistants to physicians wished to incorporate that they were allied to the grocers. However in 1617 the apothecaries were separated by Royal Charter and grocers were henceforth forbidden to keep an apothecary's shop. Throughout the rest of the seventeenth century the Society of Apothecaries grew from an original one hundred and fourteen to over a thousand, a powerful, influential and wealthy body of men. It had become a lucrative profession – so lucrative that the physicans were by now complaining publicly that their patients could not afford to buy the medicines they prescribed.

Sylvanus Bevan, in order to practise the 'art and mystery' of the apothecary within seven miles of the City, would have to have satisfied the examiners in his knowledge and election of simples and how to prepare, dispense, handle, commix and compound medicines. He would have had extensive practical experience as an apprentice in Cheapside, and would have attended the compulsory 'Simplings' of the Society which were botanical walks 'in the country, to make acquaintance with all the vegetable tribes'. These started at five a.m. in the morning from such places as Gray's Inn in Holborn, now a long way from anything more natural than a packet of frozen peas in the local supermarket.

Sylvanus was thus qualified to keep an apothecary's shop in which he could sell medicines and other remedies. Although the potential rewards were high, competition was stiff. The grocers, although prevented from selling medicines, could still sell herbs: there were druggists specializing in both the wholesale and retailing of drugs, and a growing body of chemists dispensing medicines prescribed by the physicians. In the area around Plough Court there were as many as eighteen competing businesses.

Sylvanus had all the advantages of a good Quaker. He was well trained, and possessed a good scientific mind which was of immense value in the efficient mixing of drugs. Like other Quakers, he was determined to stock goods of the best quality that he would sell at a fair price. He stamped the business with integrity in a profession that was full of charlatans playing on a gullible public, and consequently reaped the rewards of a growing clientele – many of whom no doubt were Court friends of his father-in-law.

After fifteen years of hard, successful trading, Sylvanus was joined by his brother Timothy Bevan. Timothy married in 1735 Elizabeth, daughter of the banker David Barclay of Lombard Street, a 'good' Quaker marriage in every way. Together they issued a wholesale list entitled 'A Catalogue of Druggs, and of Chemical and Galenical Medicines'. This meant that they were successful enough to be able to offer their products to other retailers. By 1731 Sylvanus was increasingly leaving the running of the business to his assistants whilst he himself concentrated on improving the wholesale business and raising his professional status. His success in the latter was confirmed when at the age of thirty-nine he was elected a Fellow of the Royal Society. He practised increasingly as a physician and wrote a number of academic treatises on anatomy, hygiene and medicine. He became a man of letters and was acquainted with most of the eminent Quakers of his time both in Britain and America, including the great William Penn.

With Sylvanus's attentions increasingly focusing elsewhere, Timothy Bevan provided continuity in the pharmacy. He had come up to London eight or nine years after Sylvanus had first opened his doors for business. He had undertaken medical training at Leyden, the great continental centre for nonconformist learning, and was to put in another five or six years under Sylvanus at Plough Court before the Society of Apothecaries would admit him to membership which took place on 6 April 1731.

Four years later he married Elizabeth Barclay and they lived together at Plough Lane for ten years before her death in 1745. He was to marry well again in 1752, this time to Hannah, daughter of the redoubtable Joseph and Hannah Gurney. Thus were united in more than just friendship three of the great Quaker families: the Bevans from Wales, the Barclays from Scotland and the Gurneys from East Anglia.

Timothy now took a house, near Sylvanus in Hackney, for his new wife. A 'sound Georgian villa . . . solid and expensive with the Quaker dread of worldly show'. Timothy Bevan was thin and sallow, plainly dressed and patently unsociable. He was never a healthy man and apparently somewhat sour in his dealings with customers.

Sylvanus Bevan died at Hackney in 1765, exactly fifty years after opening the business. Timothy, in the fashion of these family enterprises, then took into partnership his two eldest sons and changed the name to Timothy Bevan and Sons, druggists and chemists. Both sons were to be with the business but a short time. One left two years later to become a director of Barclays Bank, the other died after eight years, leaving Timothy to run the business alone again until his retirement in 1775. The son of his second marriage, Joseph Gurney Bevan, was now to take up the reins of the business.

Whilst many of the elements of the classic Quaker business enterprise were present, others were not. Certainly both Sylvanus and Timothy received rigorous apprenticeships and sound theoretical training. They were also freely exposed to progressive scientific thought. They came from a less daunting background and started their business later than some other families, such as the Lloyds. None the less the great Quaker virtues were present – their catalogue of drugs shows that many of the more dubious and often disgusting concoctions of the time were not available at Plough Court; their plain dealing and integrity is a matter of record and if Timothy was somewhat surly in his insistence on correct accounting it was at least rooted in honesty.

Taking the evolution of other Quaker enterprises as a guide, the second generation of the Bevan business would see a certain consolidation, the exhibition of sterling rather than dynamic qualities, and the careful development of the business in terms of its administration. Joseph Gurney took over the business and took up the Quaker habit of keeping the Company accounts himself. The keeping of rigorous accounts and the maintenance of meticulous, cross-indexed records are regarded as a matter of routine nowadays, to be assisted by technology wherever possible. But, in Georgian London, the general atmosphere of folly and grandeur was hardly conducive to such an attitude, still less the maintenance of such a system laboriously by hand. From the outset Joseph Gurney also established a system of keeping letters sent to clients. In fact, the client received the copy! These letters bound into periodic volumes constitute a unique record of the uninterrupted flow of a business for over sixty years.

Yet amidst a story of relative advantage comes another more typical of Quaker tolerance and honesty. Back in 1720 Sylvanus had been travelling in Cornwall and Devon. He had come across a Quaker widow, Elizabeth Cookworthy, who was in desperate financial straits. Sylvanus was anxious to help and saw promise in the eldest of her six children. Thus William Cookworthy, aged fifteen and with one coat for Sundays, made his way on foot to London to be taken into the Bevan business. He could not afford the fees to be bound as an apothecary's apprentice, yet he learnt to master Latin and Greek and the apothecary's arts. After several years he left to start up a business as a wholesale chemist and druggist in Plymouth. In 1735 he was joined in partnership by the Bevans who withdrew in 1746 when the business became known as William Cookworthy and Company. Cookworthy, in his search for new substances, discovered beds of half-decomposed kaolin-clay in Cornwall. In 1768 Cookworthy, and his partner Camelford, took out a patent, opened the Plymouth China Factory and succeeded in becoming the first maker in England of true porcelain and the founder, although no beneficiary, of a great West of England industry. In the story of Cookworthy there is the Quaker genius in applied science profiting from another Quaker virtue, the lending of a helping hand in a strictly practical sense to those in need.

Joseph, unlike his father, was a lively and outgoing man who was quick to learn. Like other substantial Quaker entrepreneurs he did not restrict himself to business activities, he was possessed of a sense of social responsibility which extended to sitting up one night a week as a Special Constable. He became, also, one of the great propagandists for the Quaker cause (known within the Society as 'Apologists'), editing a Quaker journal called *Piety Promoted* and biographies of the principal early Quakers such as Isaac Pennington and Robert Barclay.

From the time that Sylvanus established the wholesaling of drugs and other preparations, the Company had been active in America. Sylvanus Bevan and his brother supplied Amerian Friends with reliable drugs, assisted them with credit, gave them advice and generally performed personal services. When in 1751, through the prompting of Benjamin Franklin, it was resolved to establish the first British American Hospital, Sylvanus supplied the medicines which were paid for by money raised from donations in London. But the outbreak of civil war in America in 1775 meant the cessation of trade with Plough Court, particularly as Joseph Bevan's principles did not permit him to ship goods via Halifax as many traders did to get round the problem. Once the war was over orders began to flow from American druggists to the tune of several thousand pounds a year.

The next chapter of the Plough Court story concerns William Allen. Like the Bevans, the Allens were a comfortably-off Quaker family, with origins in both Nottingham and Ireland. Job Allen was a silk manufacturer in Spitalfields and William, his son born in 1770, grew up in an atmosphere of affection, security and sound religion. Although he was to spend three years in his father's silk business, his heart lay in science and whatever means he had were devoted to conducting limited experiments. A great deal of the life of this sensitive and introspective Quaker is known through a diary that he kept rigorously throughout his life. The habit of the Friends in writing everything down extended often enough to their private lives.

In 1792 Joseph Gurney Bevan offered to take William into his business. Job agreed reluctantly and young William left the silk trade to settle in at Plough Lane. At twenty-two William was no youngster to be starting out in a new business, but he still had a great deal of education to come, first attending the classes of Bryan Higgins to receive a formal education in the rudiments of science, and then, when over thirty, taking up the study of botany. He was a conscientious student in everything he undertook to study and he was later elected as a Fellow of the Linnean Society.

In those early days of formal science (the Royal Institution was formed only in 1800) it would have been relatively easy for a man of ability to make a name for himself. The Quakers with their traditional attention to detail would have been particularly respected in this area. Plough Court, with its practical, commercial outlets, became very much a centre for research and theorizing, becoming noteworthy as a repository for chemical reagents; indeed Allen himself was presented with a set by a Swiss professor. It also saw the formation of the Askean Society by young men 'desirous of improving themselves by philosophical exercises'. Each member was required to produce a scientific paper for one of the fortnightly winter meetings. Members of the Society included some of the leading young scientists of the day, including Luke Howard, William-Joseph Fox, William Pepys, Henry Lawson and, of course, William Allen. These sessions were not just talking shops, for the enthusiasm of these young men for discovery led them frequently to experiment too. 'We all breathed the gaseous oxide of azote, it took a surprising effect on one, abolishing completely all sensation . . . my eyes were fixed, my face purple . . .'. They were discovering nitrous oxide, or laughing gas.

At the end of 1803 Allen was elected one of the presidents of the Physical Society of Guy's Hospital, and through an invitation from Humphrey Davy he began a series of well over a hundred lectures on chemistry and natural philosophy at the Royal Institution. To have got thus far in so short a time was an extraordinary feat and undoubtedly he was an asset to the Plough Court business. He later became a member of the Board of Managers of the Royal Institution and a Fellow of the Royal Society. Meanwhile he did not neglect his duty to the Society, always attending meetings of Friends for both worship and business, and becoming a member of the National Annual Meeting for Sufferings. He was married twice, the second time, in 1806, to Charlotte Hanbury of Stoke Newington. He then moved to his wife's house in North London where he took charge of a household that included his wife's sister and two nephews who became like sons to him.

It is difficult to describe the stature that William Allen achieved in his life time. His authority on scientific affairs was unquestioned and widely recognized. His friends included highly placed notables including the brothers of George IV, the Dukes of York, Sussex and Cambridge. Queen Victoria's father, the Duke of Kent, was a lifetime friend, and from political circles he numbered Wilberforce, Clarkson, Babington, Lord Teignmouth, Henry Brougham and Vaux amongst regular visitors to Plough Court.

His passionate fight against slavery was marked by his fight for education. He was one of the principal supporters of Joseph Lancaster's attempts to establish schools, culminating in the establishment of the Royal Lancastrian Institution, which was to become the British and Foreign School Society, a forerunner of our present educational system. Allen also took a prominent share in the educational aspects of Robert Owen's work at New Lanark in Scotland. He finally established his own agricultural school in Sussex.

One of the more extraordinary of Allen's involvements was with the financial affairs of the Duke of Kent. The Duke had pressing financial problems, partly of his own making. By 1815 these threatened to leave him in a humiliating position. Allen became one of the two trusteees the Duke agreed should handle his personal affairs which included administering his estate when the Duke died in 1820, eight months after the birth of his daughter – the heir to the throne, Queen Victoria.

Allen travelled extensively in Europe and Russia where he established a personal relationship with Czar Alexander I. In 1797, by which time he was the principal of the Company, he took into partnership Luke Howard, a man much his own age. He was the son of Robert Howard, a founder of the Bible Society. Young Luke had been to school in Burford, Oxfordshire – to that very same school run by Thomas Huntley, where biscuits were first baked and sold by Mrs Huntley. After that he served his apprenticeship in Stockport with a pharmaceutical chemist before joining a London firm of wholesale druggists. He had also run his own chemist shop in Temple Bar.

Allen and Howard got on very well and their partnership was a happy if short one. Luke Howard had a flair for making heavy chemicals. By now the business had a chemical factory in Plaistow and Luke Howard took charge of it, William Allen remaining at Plough Court to run the laboratory and the retail business. Their partnership was dissolved in 1806 with no bad feeling. The two aspects of the business had developed to the point where each required the undivided attention of the respective partner. For the next ten years William Allen ran the business under his own name, the pharmacy gaining a reputation for the wide range of its products. These included such preparations as Confectio Damocratis, a confection like Venice Treacle, pure pharmaceuticals, as well as standard chemicals that iron foundries and other establishments were needing in increasing quantities.

One of the principal employees of the period was John Barry. He became responsible for many of the internal affairs of the Company including control of the laboratory. He also reorganized the retail side of the business paying particular care to the dispensing department. He was something of a disciplinarian, fixing the shape of the bottles on the shelves, demanding exact time-keeping by his staff, and even insisting on his assistants' recording where they attended church on Sundays.

Life at Plough Court was certainly rigorous, the twelve-hour day a long one and the work hard. Yet there were four meals a day, even for the warehouse assistant who literally slept under the counter. The employees had a sitting room over the warehouse next door at No. 3 Plough Court and a housekeeper to look after them.

John Barry gave most of his time to running the establishment and yet was able to concentrate on applying his considerable mechanical ability. In 1819 he patented a vacuum apparatus which was to be used for the separation of ingredients in medicinal extraction. He was also an active Quaker who spent much of his precious spare time seeking the abolition of the death penalty. He had an intimate knowledge of parliamentary procedure which was enormously helpful to William Allen in his campaigns. Unfortunately he was to die at the relatively young age of forty-three in 1832, the victim of a laboratory explosion which serves to remind us that the conditions under which science was conducted in the nineteenth century were far from safe, and that progress was sometimes achieved at the expense of tragic losses of life.

By this time William Allen himself was approaching the last ten years of his life. They were to be spent in undertaking the responsibilities that his eminent status had thrust upon him. He always saw his prime duty as being to the Society of Friends. Despite his association with Royalty he never accepted a purely social invitation from his associates at Court. He spent much of his time during these final years in travelling on the Continent and in correspondence with notables who could help his various causes.

He died on 30 December 1843 at Lindfield in Sussex. His obituary mentions his membership of the Astronomical Society and the Royal Society, his professorship of Experimental Philosophy at Guy's Hospital, his knowledge of astronomy and his general combination of sound knowledge, suavity of manners and sterling principles. His life was devoted to the best interests of mankind, to the well-being of the Society of Friends and to the continued growth of the enterprise at Plough Court.

The Hanburys who came from Hanbury in Worcestershire, like the Bevans and the Allens, were of ancient and influential stock, achieving distinction in many walks of life, not least in business. In 1642 John Hanbury, as a result of his staunch support of Parliament, had fled his Worcestershire home to escape the plundering Royalists. He had acquired through inheritance, an interest in an ironworks in Pontypool in Monmouth. He was a 'dealer in merchandise of iron'. His grandson inherited the business in Wales and was the first man in the world to develop the technique of rolling iron plates rather than hammering them down.

However, it was John Hanbury's younger brother who first joined the Society of Friends. His grandson, Capel Hanbury, achieved prominence as a soap merchant in Bristol. Two generations later his granddaughter, Charlotte Hanbury, married William Allen. The names of Allen and Hanbury were thus linked and another Quaker dynasty was born.

Daniel Bell Hanbury was not their child but their nephew, being the son of Charlotte's elder brother, Capel Hanbury III. He grew up in Stamford Hill in North London and received a meagre education in Tottenham. His father had been reduced in circumstances because of business reverses and so Daniel was sent to work in 1808 at Plough Court, although apparently he was never formally apprenticed, and developed a life-long interest in dispensing.

He was joined six years later by his brother Cornelius, a lively and good-humoured young man. He was formally apprenticed to learn the 'art of chemist and druggist' and it is worth wondering why he was indentured and not his brother. At first he was put to work in the counting house, although like all the apprentices he would be given experience of the shop, warehouse and laboratory as well.

Daniel and Cornelius lived with their Uncle William and Aunt Charlotte in the Stoke Newington home. In 1822, at the age of twenty-six Cornelius married William Allen's daughter Mary. It was a tragically short-lived liaison as Mary was to die the following year giving birth to a son, William Allen Hanbury. The two boys were admitted in 1824 to partnership in the business and the Company was renamed Allen, Hanburys and Barry. By this time Allen was in his mid-fifties and was increasingly away from the business, John Barry effectively administering the enterprise. Daniel concerned himself with the shop whilst Cornelius looked after the counting house.

Cornelius was to develop a life-long concern for the victims of accidents and was therefore typical of nineteenth-century Quakers who generally developed a specific area of social or philanthropic interest and spent their life, money and influence in its pursuit.

Thus, through marriage and apprenticeship the Hanburys found their way into a business begun by the Bevans and inherited by the Allens. Although Cornelius and his eldest brother, Daniel, made true contributions to the business at Plough Lane, it was Cornelius's son, Cornelius II, who was to have the profoundest effect on the fortunes of Allen and Hanbury. As both family and business were substantially successful, young Cornelius was certainly well placed in life. He received private tuition in a room on the top floor of Plough Court, driving there each day in his father's carriage. It was decided that he should qualify as both a surgeon and an apothecary. He was therefore apprenticed to a surgeon-apothecary in Bishopsgate for five years. During this time he also became a student at St Bartholomew's Hospital, qualifying as a surgeon in 1849 and as an apothecary in 1850.

In 1850 he married Sarah Janson, the daughter of a Lloyds' underwriter, and began to attend to the daily business at Plough Court. He was joined by his cousin Daniel, the son of one of the two nephews brought up in William Allen's home and a qualified pharmaceutical chemist with an outstanding knowledge of botany and materia medica. Together they ran the business for fifteen years.

Their first step was to effect substantial alterations to No. 2 Plough Court. The shop was enlarged and three small windows were replaced with one large one. Two oval panels were set into the glass displaying the arms of the Apothecaries' Society and of the Pharmaceutical Society. A new counter was fitted with five dispensing stations. A speaking-tube now linked the ground and first floors, ventilation was improved, and special attention was given to the display of medicine chests. Building changes in Lombard Street caused further structural alteration in 1872. The old premises were reluctantly pulled down and re-erected on the same site but with a different aspect. The new premises contained the pharmacy on the ground floor. An old mahogany counter, shaped like a horseshoe, extended practically round the entire interior, the drugs being arrayed on mahogany shelves behind. The public floor-space was dominated by a double settee, also in mahogany, and six Georgian oak chairs. On the right of the ground floor was the surgical department, preparing orders for dressings and surgical sundries. The laboratories were now situated on the third floor.

Cornelius was aware of the great commercial expansion happening everywhere and the steady growth in demand for drugs. He also wanted to manufacture certain of their own medicinal specialities. Three years later when Daniel left the business in 1871 he determined to lease a factory in Bethnal Green, then a semi-rural area east of London. It was one of a group of small factories manufacturing such things as matches, mineral waters and disinfectant. Cornelius took over the match factory as the initial acquisition in a process that would take over thirty years before all the factories were obtained by the Company. This meant a gradual process of transferring the manufacturing and wholesale work from Plough Court. Cornelius was based in the City and the new complex was looked after by his son Frederick, with the assistance of the able William Dodd, a pharmaceutical chemist. It was no easy task converting the scattered buildings at Bethnal Green into the nucleus of a factory, and the application of mechanics to the manufacturing process was still at the 'Heath Robinson' stage.

Cornelius was also interested in the manufacture of surgical instruments and he installed a small forge and workshop at Bethnal Green. Eventually in the early part of this century a factory was erected for this purpose.

In 1894 the Company opened premises at Wigmore Street to act as showrooms and the manufacture of specially ordered surgical appliances. Another pharmacy had already been opened at Vere Street where the development of new medicinal preparations took place, including 'Chrimsol' (liquid paraffin), 'Saverin' (a bacillus) and a liquid preparation for treating thyroid problems.

By the turn of the century it was evident that the factory at Bethnal Green was insufficient to meet the growing demands of their business. In 1898 a site on the banks of the Lea at Ware in Hertfordshire was acquired. Initially six people worked at Ware compared to over 900 in 1950. Tall malt buildings were constructed followed by extensive workshops. The manufacture of goods and malted products was transferred to the new factory, and in 1900 that of pastilles and capsules.

Entering the twentieth century Allen and Hanburys ceased to be a Quaker family enterprise. In 1893 Allen and Hanburys had been incorporated with an authorized capital of £75,000. The new Company purchased the assets from Cornelius and Frederick Hanbury for £20,000 in ordinary shares, and £40,000 in preference shares. Sixty years later the authorized capital was £1,000,000. Once again the private family venture became inadequate and ultimately obsolete. Cornelius, too, had gone the way of the third generation Quaker entrepreneur; he had grown up in comfort and success, identified more with the Establishment than with nonconformism and he had joined the Church of England, a pattern that was all too common with the Quaker businesses.

Allen and Hanbury today is a Company of international ramifications. It began like so many Quaker ventures with the enterprise of a single individual who was able to combine a spirit of enquiry and a passion for knowledge with a capacity for hard, honest endeavour. The story of Allen and Hanburys is truly a story of 'critical' individuals: Sylvanus Bevan, William Allen, Daniel Hanbury and Cornelius Hanbury. Each contributed to the full their immense capabilities. The pharmacy turned out no less than five Fellows of the Royal Society. The role of the Company and its employees in the development of pharmaceutical science in creating a healthier world can scarcely be denied; it has been a role as critical as, say, that of the Darbys in ironmaking, the Lloyds in banking or the Rowntrees in cocoa.

CHAPTER 10

The Friendly Enterprise: Conclusion

In looking at the scope of Quaker enterprise, and in detail at that of individual families, one is led to the conclusion that there was no magic 'ingredient' to explain the unique success of the Friends in business. As fast as one element is identified as being crucial to the success of one enterprise it is found to be notably lacking in the story of another.

Unlike other religious minorities such as the Jews, the Quakers had no tribal instinct, no historic ethic to guide them. In fact, comparisons with most other minorities is superficial for the Friends went out into the community to find their success rather than withdrew from it and whilst, like other minorities, the Quakers had strictures relating to codes of behaviour, 'marrying out' and answerability, the Friends were never self-serving in their business, philanthropy or social commitment.

The Quakers certainly possessed one common quality in abundance – they were imbued with the so-called 'Protestant ethic', as described by Weber, that was so closely allied to the development of capitalism – work was seen as an end in itself, worth doing for its own sake, good for the soul. Honesty, plain dealing and worthiness were to be admired; ostentation and personal materialism avoided. Clearly the virtues inherent in the Calvinistic outlook were very good for business but this again is no explanation for the ethic was commonly held throughout Victorian society and whilst, perhaps, the Quakers were a little more sincere and less hypocritical there is no doubt that these virtues were publicly held to be desirable.

Another possible explanation would be that the Quakers came of a particular stock, or region, or culture but in fact this is not so. Many of the early Friends were, admittedly, of yeomen stock and had about them the fierce independence and common sense of that type. George Fox, himself, came of such stock and certainly families such as the Crosfields and the Palmers shared this origin. Yet others, equally influential in the Society, came from families with considerable histories of influence and privilege. The Lloyds are a good example as was of course one of the other founders, William Penn. Such families often had to trade heavily on their connections in the difficult early years of the Society when persecution was at its height. It may well be that the strong pragmatic instincts of the Friends evolved from the influence of such families within the society. It must often have meant survival.

Again, neither of these roots had any tradition to explain the development of a mature ideology which has, in fact, remained intact and withstood intellectual challenge until the present day. The philosophy of the Friends, with its emphasis on individual conscience and determination, was born among the ideological refugees from both orthodox Puritanism particularly in its most extreme form in Presbyterian Scotland, and the inherent corruption of Church and State rolled into one in the form of the English Stuart monarchy. Men like David Barclay coming from the professional, educated middle class gave the philosophy of the Society its definition and its predilection for knowledge and understanding – for that way lay freedom.

Landed gentry, yeomen, professional classes – these were pretty well the backgrounds of pre-industrial England in general and certainly were not peculiar to the Society. In much the same way it can be shown that there was no real commonality of occupation or activity and if they came to dominate areas like provincial banking, ironmaking, or the manufacture of chocolate it was because they developed these activities rather than just colonized them.

It is also important to reject the notion that the Quakers were simply 'in the right place at the right time'. The vast opportunities offered by the Industrial Revolution with its associated opportunities for overseas colonization and trade were available to everyone in a position to take advantage of them and there were many groups within English society that were better placed than a small sect of socially undesirable moralists.

So we are still left with the question why?

It is possible that whilst the elements of Quaker success were not unique, or even held in common by all businesses, the particular combination of these elements was unique. Moreover the fact that the Quakers had as a group no 'pre-history' before the period in question meant that their resources as a group were born of that time and were of it. Having no tradition, no outworn or irrelevant codes, the Friends were able to take full advantage of their opportunities to the point that the momentum they created became self-sustaining.

What happened, therefore, was the dream of every modern monopolist. The Quakers developed a set of interacting elements where everything assisted everything else in a progressively more refined manner to the point where the product of these elements infinitely outweighed their sum. Through this set of interacting elements the Quakers were able to create enterprises of unique force in Victorian society. It is worth reviewing, again, some of these elements.

The particular organization of the Society was again entirely of assistance in this process. The self-protecting lack of both hierarchy and centralization, the non-secularization of meetings and centres, the strongly autonomous and independent nature of each group meant that they carried no unwieldy bureaucracy, or doctrine through which progress had to be filtered and ultimately checked.

This is not to say that the Society had no strength, no power to influence or control members. The ethics of the Society were minuted in a series of advices to members and the fact that individuals entered voluntarily into their commitment and held it without the application of sanctions made the bond, in some ways, that much stronger. It was not, therefore, simply a question of 'obeying the rules', it was more a case that there was no point in remaining a Quaker if the ethics were unacceptable. Thus it was that members quite voluntarily allowed themselves to be called to account for their business affairs and have their accounts inspected for indebtedness and good practice, if either were felt to be at risk. Members knew that whilst such procedures undoubtedly helped protect the Society from the risks of external criticism it was also done out of love and concern. When, in fact, members were found to be deficient then it was the duty of other Friends to help them out of their difficulties. In this way the Society was tremendously supportive of Friends in business – an important element in the psychology of any new enterprise.

Membership of the Society, *per se*, had other advantages as we have mentioned from time to time. The practice of not marrying 'out' was not unique and has been a feature of virtually every religious grouping particularly the extreme nonconformist sects such as the Mormons, non-Christian groups such as Muslims and Jews, and even Catholics. The psychology of this seems self-evident and it is also an important means for survival through regeneration. Given the fact that before the Limited Liability Acts, personal liability meant keeping control of the business 'in the family', then the best way of extending the business, acquiring new capital, partners, or fresh blood for management was through marriage to another business family. As we know, in banking and the iron industry in particular, whole strings of businesses were effected by the Quakers through partnerships formed as a result of well thought-out marriages. The fact that the Friends were also extremely productive meant many such marriages were possible.

The Quakers were not unique in this. The peculiar intensity of this process amongst Quakers is probably best explained by two things: 'intervisitation' and 'innovation'.

The persecution of the Friends and their sufferings which were minutely recorded at local, regional and national levels meant that a strong tradition of intervisitation developed from the start to support and comfort Friends in the hours of their difficulties. The peculiarly autonomous nature of individual 'meetings' meant that there was no centralized communications structure through which information could pass and again intervisitation became the important means through which news of developments could be carried from group to group. There was continuous movement from one group to another carrying ideas and forging new relationships.

The preclusion of Friends from the professions forced them into other activities, and like other excluded minorities they often sought refuge in the safety of their own minds and began a tradition of intellectual approach within their own Society. This approach was channelled away from 'academia' and into the new and developing area of the applied sciences, the practical applications of which were fodder for the new Quaker businesses. Thus the Quakers were ideally placed to ride the tide of opportunity presented by the Industrial Revolution and the commercial explosion which followed it. There were, however, many others who were similarly placed but the difference, the uniqueness of the Quaker position, lay in the combination of intervisitation and innovation. Through this, an intensity of action developed in key areas such as iron-working and country banking that became self-sustaining.

It is an old adage that whilst men may trap other men's bodies through imprisonment, relieve them of their social and economic resources and outwardly force them to accept both ideology and modes of conduct, they can never hope to capture their minds. Oppressed or socially unacceptable groups have therefore sought refuge in contemplation and philosophy. The very act of silence that has become the trade mark of Quaker worship, whilst born of a defensive necessity to avoid giving any more excuse for their persecution than could be helped, quickly became a value in itself. Unlike other minorities, the Quakers had no access to the universities as teachers and consequently their understanding developed as 'knowledge' rather than theory or philosophy. Through deep thought the Quakers came to value understanding, and the opportunities and freedom that knowledge gave them. They developed a heavy emphasis on the education of their young, and their insistence that members of the family backed this knowledge with a thorough apprenticeship meant a continuity of management know-how and attitude over three or four generations.

Were the Quakers a 'Mafia'? There is a tendency to think of them as some sort of self-perpetuating masonic group interested only in scratching each others' backs. Loud was the complaint, for example, in Bristol that only the Quakers had kettles. The closely interlocked set of partnerships stitched across whole areas of activity would have given a powerful impression of the 'hidden hand' of conspiracy. It is a criticism that evolved, however, after the event as a shorthand attempt to dismiss Quaker success.

It would be true that Quakers no doubt preferred doing business with each other and that family and social connections would have eased the path of business between them, but there is no evidence that they ever did each other particular favours. Indeed the Society would have frowned heavily on anything less than the maintenance of strict business ethics in dealings between Friends. Nor is there any evidence, as there is with other minorities, that 'outsiders' were deliberately excluded in favour of dealings with Friends. As we have said, the Quakers went out into the world rather than withdrawing from it and their economic, social and philanthropic achievements were in the real world and not within carefully selected parts of it. Of course, when it came to borrowing money a Quaker banker would be favourably disposed towards another Friend but not simply because they shared membership of the Society but because he would know that there was every chance that the client was honest, liable to repay his debts, and likely to conduct his business affairs in a way that gave reasonable opportunities to create enough money to service the debt. Similar considerations must have operated when it came to speculation in canals, railways and other public schemes. Final proof that this was no closed group exploiting society comes with the endless examples of Quakers being asked by non-Quakers to act as treasurers or secretaries to public ventures.

One wonders what those sepia-tinted gentlemen thought of their own success. What would the Barclays, the Bevans, the Buxtons, the Huntleys, the Palmers, Rowntrees, Cadburys and Frys, the Terrys and Jacobs, the Crosfields, Wedgwoods, Wilkinsons, and so many others, have wanted said of their achievements? As members of a Society having as its basis a moral attitude to life, they would probably prefer accounts to be couched in ethical terms rather than modern business jargon. The term 'enlightened self-interest' comes frequently to mind, and perhaps that is where the link between business and ethic lies in this analysis.

The Quakers were, during the eighteenth and nineteenth centuries, a Society of plain dealing, worthy and honest people. They were probably rather too much so for contemporary digestion. Their strong sense of individualism led logically to an automatic respect for the essential rights and dignity of others. So they saw the necessity for freedom through education and knowledge, for decent working conditions for employees, for human relations based on respect at work, and for the alleviation of poverty and suffering through the raising of living standards. These tendencies were not only desirable in themselves but also good for business. Clean, healthy, working conditions, a general sense of purpose fostered through good work relations, and an absence of disease and poverty on the part of the employees led to efficient, profitable production. Allied to the Quakers' carefully acquired 'know-how', their rigorous attention to record keeping and accounting, and above all their honest, straightforward dealings with their clients, made a considerable impact during a period when economic and social revolution was creating vast opportunities for those able to exploit them.

We have seen that the Quaker family enterprise was more than equipped to succeed during this period. Eventually these family Companies became victims of their own success, became too big to be sustained by the family unit, too successful to maintain the simple principles on which they had been developed. The coming of limited liability and the injection of external, disinterested capital, was the death-knell of the family business. The names live on, however, in today's monster Companies, and many of those early principles are still to be found in part in the general attitude of these ventures. Although the Quaker business is part of the history of the last two centuries, it has certainly left its mark upon this one.

Index